# Destination
# PRIDE

Andrew Collins

Illustrations by Wenjia Tang

Hardie Grant

EXPLORE

# Contents

# Introduction

What is gay travel to you? Is it going some place with campy bars and pulsing clubs where you can meet and flirt with lots of other LGBTQ people? Or is it travelling to Pride festivals, lesbian dance parties, drag shows, gay ski weeks and other social events? Perhaps for you it's more about experiencing a relaxing, romantic vacation with your boo and being able to hold hands and canoodle without having to endure judgy stares. Maybe it's visiting places that have a queer, creative energy — fantastic theatres, swanky design shops, boho cafes, amazing art museums and indie cinemas. Or is it seeking out an inclusive, sex-positive vibe — perhaps staying in a clothing-optional guest house or close to gay beaches and saunas?

•

These are just a few of the responses I've heard over the three decades I've been writing about gay travel. And, not infrequently, I hear an answer like this: being gay isn't a big factor in my travels. I just want to go wherever I feel like going and be treated like anybody else.

Perhaps you can relate to most or maybe even all of these answers. I know I can. Mostly I travel with my partner, but sometimes I go it alone or with other friends. Many of the trips I've taken over the years – 4th of July weekend on Fire Island, Pride week in Taipei – have felt gay with a capital G. Others – like the time I spent ten days milling around stodgy, patrician resorts in the south-eastern US to research a story for a golf magazine – not so much. As I said to a friend at the time, 'I guess it qualified as gay travel. I was travelling, and I'm gay. But only barely.'

That's the thing about gay travel. It's a bit slippery to define exactly, but if you're LGBTQ and you've ever gone on holiday, you undoubtedly have some ideas about how gay and mainstream travel differ from one another. For most of us, identifying as a sexual minority affects how we experience the world around us, and what we're looking for on vacation.

As a travel writer, what makes me happiest is that the number of places popular with gay travellers has exploded over the past couple of decades. Queer people are no longer relegated to choosing our next holiday destination from among a handful of famously tolerant towns and cities.

This isn't to say I don't love visiting the world's iconic LGBTQ destinations – London, San Francisco, Toronto and the like. It's just that I also greatly enjoy discovering and writing about less-obvious places with emerging gay scenes, such as Colombia, Estonia and India. Or compelling destinations that may not be particularly progressive but offer lots of other charms – the stunning national parks of southern Utah and the splendid museums of Istanbul, for instance. And I've always had a soft spot for exploring quirky small towns, underrated cities and remote places with unexpectedly robust queer communities – I'm thinking of Salt Spring Island in western Canada, the Blue Mountains outside Sydney, the offbeat West Texas town of Marfa. Although often regionally famous, these offbeat or off-the-beaten-path destinations aren't usually well-known internationally.

*Destination Pride* takes you to all of these fabulous places and many more. My inclusion of different parts of the world is by no means exhaustive, but I have tried to include a mix of both classic and surprising points of queer interest.

It seems remarkable to make this claim more than a year into the COVID-19 pandemic, a situation that has presented us all with myriad travel challenges: but this may very well be the best moment in history for LGBTQ people to explore the planet. While there's still a great need for further progress, especially regarding transgender rights, support for queer people has never been greater. As borders reopen and we resume our holiday plans, now is a perfect time to travel the globe, whether that means happily meandering with your partner along a tranquil tropical beach or partying with a few hundred new friends till dawn on a gay cruise around the Mediterranean. Follow your queer wanderlust!

**A word about words:** The language we use to describe ourselves and express our identities is forever evolving. I've used the acronym LGBTQ as well as the words 'gay' and 'queer' interchangeably throughout this book to refer generally to any of us who identify as lesbian, gay male, bisexual, transgender, questioning, intersex, asexual, ally, nonbinary and gender nonconforming. And I've used more specific terms – lesbian, gay male, transgender – where context warrants it.

# Iconic LGBTQ destinations

If you're reading this book, you
don't need me to tell you that
San Francisco and London have
huge, vibrant queer scenes. You might
be more surprised to learn about
less obvious LGBTQ destinations
such as Mumbai or Guadalajara, in
which case, keep reading — you'll
find them in later chapters.

But in this chapter, in discussing the world's unofficial LGBTQ capitals, I've decided to focus less on the 'why go' and instead answer the following question: Which experiences should be on my bucket list when I visit the world's gay meccas?

Before I recommend what to do and see in what I've deemed the 'seven urban gay wonders of the world', I'll confess that any list like this is inherently a little arbitrary. I could easily have expanded it to 10 or even 20 cities. I considered several others: Bangkok, Los Angeles, Berlin, Tel Aviv, Amsterdam, Chicago, Madrid, Vancouver, Miami and – the place I live and love – Mexico City. In the end, I found other places in the book to talk about these and well over a hundred other towns and cities.

So here we go, the big seven. There's enough to delight you for days or even weeks in all of these large, bustling cities. I've included the five things to see or do (in no particular order) to put at the top of your list.

## BARCELONA

As different as Barcelona and Madrid are from one another, either of these thriving, sophisticated Spanish cities deserved to be on this list. But I give Barcelona a slight edge because of its spectacular Mediterranean setting, sunny climate, gorgeous Modernista architecture and astonishingly good food and wine (to be sure, Madrid is no slouch either). Also, Barcelona is an easy 30-minute train ride to a fantastic LGBTQ beach town, Sitges, with its own lively seaside promenade, stately mansions, fine art galleries, and friendly gay bars and cafes.

## THE BUCKET LIST

**Marvel** at Antoni Gaudí's architecture, especially Sagrada Família and Park Güell.

**Saunter** among the lively gay clubs and tapas bars of the elegant Eixample (aka 'Gaixample') neighbourhood.

**Laze** on the gay beach at Barceloneta.

**Ride** the funicular railway to Montjuïc Park and visit its castle and Fundació Miró, the art museum dedicated to modern Spanish master Joan Miró.

**Take** to the cobblestone streets of the Gothic Quarter, with its medieval buildings and eclectic museums.

## LONDON

For many gay travellers, this 2000-year-old Roman city is Europe's foremost destination, a constantly evolving and exciting whirr of diversity, and a trendsetter in queer-sensible fashion, film, theatre, art and music. Try to visit in spring or summer, when parks and gardens are in bloom – the hugely attended London Pride festival is in late June. One of the world's great museum cities, London has also transformed its once staid dining scene into one of Europe's most exciting.

## THE BUCKET LIST

**Partake** of the festive LGBTQ nightlife, buzzy restaurants, fashionable Carnaby Street shopping, and esteemed theatres of Soho and the West End.

**Stroll** the literary lanes of Bloomsbury and Russell Square, with a stop at famed Gay's The Word bookstore and a visit to the British Museum.

**Enjoy** nature – and people-watching – in cruisey and expansive Hampstead Heath park, especially its bath ponds, which have separate female and male sections, and West Heath areas.

**Admire** the many renowned attractions and bridges along both banks of the Thames, from Westminster Abbey and the Tower of London to the London Eye and the Tate Modern.

**Wander** about London's happening and youthful up-and-coming queer-approved neighbourhoods, including Hackney, Shoreditch, Dalston and Stoke Newington.

LGBTQ people have flocked to the largest city in the United States for well over a century. But it wasn't until a sultry June night in 1969, when a group of mostly marginalised queer folks – many of them people of colour and transgender – became fed up with chronic police harassment and staged a riot at a bar called the Stonewall Inn, that the entire world noticed New York City's vital, and not to be silenced, gay community. This city of 8.5 million is dynamic, exciting, sophisticated and still as conspicuously queer as ever. Midtown down to lower Manhattan may be where visitors spend most of their time, but more recently much of the city's excitement – and LGBTQ scene – has migrated north to Harlem and Washington Heights, and across the East River to various parts of Brooklyn and, increasingly, Queens.

## THE BUCKET LIST

**Walk** along the linear High Line park and then tour the superb Whitney Museum of American Art before exploring uber-queer Chelsea and the West Village.

**See** a big-name musical on Broadway and go gay-bar-hopping afterwards in neighbouring Hells Kitchen.

**Tour** the extraordinary cultural institutions of Museum Mile, especially the Metropolitan Museum of Art and the Cooper Hewitt Smithsonian Design Museum.

**Spend** a day visiting hip and historic Brooklyn's most charming and LGBTQ-popular neighbourhoods, including lesbian-centric Park Slope and the Brooklyn Museum in neighbouring Prospect Park, and the stellar food and craft-beer scenes in Williamsburg, Greenpoint and Bushwick.

**Get** your fix of sunshine at busy but beautiful Central Park or the more off-the-beaten-path Met Cloisters and Fort Tryon Park.

The combination of its dramatic natural setting and an inspiring, poignant LGBTQ history has made the City by the Bay arguably the mecca of gay meccas. There's something self-consciously showy about San Francisco's landmarks and attractions – the clanging cable cars, the orange piers of Golden Gate Bridge, the riotously colourful 'painted lady' Victorian houses, the barking sea lions of Pier 39. It's a city that basks in the spotlight, right down to the giant rainbow flags that fly high above the steep streets of the Castro District. San Francisco is simultaneously old-fashioned and cutting-edge, a leader in contemporary art, inventive cuisine and progressive politics. It's also a beach getaway, albeit with a chillier climate (and downright frigid waters – pack a wetsuit if you plan on swimming).

## THE BUCKET LIST

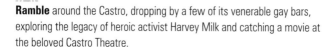

**Ramble** around the Castro, dropping by a few of its venerable gay bars, exploring the legacy of heroic activist Harvey Milk and catching a movie at the beloved Castro Theatre.

**Visit** the greenery and compelling attractions of Golden Gate Park – including de Young Museum, California Academy of Sciences and San Francisco Botanical Garden – and the rugged ocean cliffs nearby at Lands End.

**View** the exhibits at the outstanding San Francisco Museum of Modern Art before walking around the trendy SoMa warehouse district and visiting its queer bars.

**Explore** the celebrated restaurant and bar scene of the Mission District, a diverse mix of Latino, feminist, LGBTQ, Asian and hipster culture.

**Buy** picnic supplies from the gourmet vendors inside the Ferry Terminal Building and catch a ferry across the bay to Sausalito or – from Pier 33, a little further north – a tour boat to Alcatraz Island.

## SÃO PAULO

The most populous city in both the Western and Southern hemispheres, this cosmopolitan blend of cultures – it claims some of the world's largest Jewish, Italian, Japanese and North African populations – also boasts Latin America's largest and most visible LGBTQ community. In early June, as many as five million people attend the city's annual Pride parade. Its seaside sibling, Rio de Janeiro, is arguably Brazil's greater gay tourism draw thanks to its incomparable beach culture, but São Paulo is a world-class centre of gastronomy and design.

## THE BUCKET LIST

**Party** away in the pulsing gay clubs and sceney bars of Frei Caneca Street.

**Soak** up the scenery and culture of Oscar Niemeyer–designed Parque Ibirapuera, including the outstanding Museu Afro Brasil and São Paulo Museum of Modern Art.

**Check** out the hipster retail and cafe scene in the queer-popular Pinheiros district, including the vibrant Saturday market at Praça Benedito Calixto.

**Sip** caipirinhas and enjoy the views of the city's dazzling skyline at Skye Bar or one of the city's many other trendy rooftop venues.

**Shop** among the swanky high-end fashion shops of exclusive Jardim Paulista.

## SYDNEY

For many LGBTQ travellers, attending the rollicking Sydney Gay and Lesbian Mardi Gras is a dream fulfilled. And while it absolutely should be, especially if you love to party, visiting Sydney is an immense pleasure any time of year. The spectacular waterfront setting – from picturesque Sydney Harbour to a coast lined with dozens of marvellous beaches – is just part of the appeal. With its welcoming spirit, Sydney has long been an LGBTQ go-to for its bubbly nightlife scene and eclectic neighbourhoods. And then there's the amazing culinary offerings.

## THE BUCKET LIST

**Explore** the harbour, from the iconic Sydney Opera House to the stylish Rocks district to booking a Sydney Harbour Bridge Climb (if you're okay with heights, that is).

**Dance** and drink the night away at the many gay pubs and clubs on Oxford Street in Darlinghurst.

**Enjoy** the foodie-driven restaurants and indie shopping of LGBTQ-popular inner suburbs such as Newtown and Erskineville.

**Have** brunch on a cafe terrace in this city that popularised avocado toast and is known for top-notch coffee, ethereal baked goods and fresh-squeezed fruit juices.

**Walk** the Bondi to Bronte coastal path and then sunbathe and swim at Bondi Beach – don't miss the queer-popular section on the north-east side of the crescent.

## TORONTO

Although it has always been Canada's business and cultural centre, this sprawling lakefront metropolis endured a rather staid reputation up to the 1970s. In the past half-century, however, Toronto has received a serious infusion of energy and excitement, thanks in part to a massive influx of immigrants from all over the world. More than half of its nearly three million residents were born outside of Canada, a fact that's easy to appreciate by exploring its many international neighbourhoods (and exceptional globally influenced restaurants and shops). Toronto boasts the country's largest LGBTQ community and hosts one of the world's best-attended Pride festivals.

CHURCH · WELLESLEY

VILLAGE

Church St.

484

## THE BUCKET LIST

**Stroll** amid the indie shops and hipster eateries of diverse and queer-centric West Queen West on the west side and Leslieville (affectionately known as 'Lesbianville') on the east side.

**Flirt**, dance and mingle in the many bars and cafes of lively Church Street Gay Village.

**Ride** a ferry boat to the Toronto Islands, and sunbathe on the sand at queer-popular, clothing-optional Hanlan's Point before walking among the gardens and amusements of Centre Island.

**Explore** the fascinating galleries and world-class travelling exhibitions at the Royal Ontario Museum, the Art Gallery of Ontario and the lesser-known but remarkable Bata Shoe Museum.

**Take** in the skyline and lakefront from the 553-metre-high (1814-foot-high) observation deck of the CN Tower – and, for the ultimate adrenaline rush, book an EdgeWalk.

# It takes a village

One thing that all iconic gay cities have in common is having at least one prominent neighbourhood with an explicitly LGBTQ identity — a gay village, gaybourhood, gay ghetto or whatever else you might call it. These dense and dynamic concentrations of bars, shops, restaurants and other businesses owned by or that cater heavily to queer people have given the world's leading LGBTQ cities their inclusive, creative identities.

Some cities — New York City and London, for example — have more than one gay district. Some of these villages are popular to live and work in, while others are mostly about bars and entertainment. Some stretch for blocks and blocks, and others are as compact as a single intersection with a gay bar or a lesbian-owned cafe and an LGBTQ community centre. Whatever their characteristics, when you want to quickly tap into the local gay scene, these lively neighbourhoods are the best places to start.

·

In addition to the others mentioned in this chapter, here's a sampling of vibrant gay villages to explore in your travels:

- **Canal Street**, Manchester (*see* p. 45)
- **Chueca**, Madrid (*see* p. 66)
- **Davie Village** and **Commercial Drive**, Vancouver (*see* p. 61)
- **The Gayborhood**, Philadelphia (*see* p. 73)
- **Gay Village**, Montréal (*see* p. 136)
- **Hillcrest**, San Diego
- **Lakeview** (aka 'Boystown') and **Andersonville**, Chicago (*see* p. 42)
- **Midtown**, Atlanta
- **Montrose**, Houston
- **Schöneberg**, Berlin (*see* p. 42)
- **Shinjuku Ni-chōme**, Tokyo (*see* p. 68).

# Celebrating romance

.

Travel and romance go hand-in-hand.
Or, rather, travelling someplace where
you and the one you love can happily
stroll hand-in-hand is paramount
to an enjoyable trip. Fortunately,
the portion of the world that's gay-
affirming, and where queer couples
can be affectionate in public,
keeps growing.

Beyond being safe and welcoming, what makes a destination romantic? That depends entirely on you – it might mean creature comforts, like plush hotel rooms with fireplaces and cosy bistros. It could simply be the chance to loll around together on a secluded beach, far from honking horns and mobile phones. Or, possibly, it's going somewhere to tie the knot or celebrate an anniversary together. The options are endless.

## WHERE TO CELEBRATE YOUR LOVE

Among those endless options, here are
some standouts.

**Aoraki/Mount Cook National Park**
This awesome landscape on the South Island is
famous for its shimmering glacial peaks, including
New Zealand's highest point, 3724-metre
(12,218-foot) Aoraki/Mount Cook. It's an
incredible setting for getting hitched. Minutes
after your ceremony, a helicopter can whisk you
away for snowshoeing across a glacier, exploring
an ice cave or skiing down a stunning slope of
fresh powder – wedding planners in these parts
can arrange just about any extreme adventure.
Or, if promising to spend the rest of your life
with someone sounds extreme enough, you can
just bliss out with a bottle of champagne in your
luxury villa overlooking the rippling waters of
Lake Pukaki.

> Wedding
> planners in
> these parts
> can arrange
> just about
> any extreme
> adventure.

## Cinque Terre and Amalfi

Although these two regions along Italy's western coast lie approximately 700 kilometres (430 miles) apart, they both have incredible scenery and romantic cliffside inns. To the north between Florence and Genoa, Cinque Terre comprises five ancient fishing villages. Though less over-the-top luxurious than the Amalfi Coast, it still offers some magical lodgings, such as the Grand Hotel Portovenere, which occupies a former monastery. In the south, just beyond the Sorrento Peninsula from Pompei and Naples, the swanky Amalfi Coast has dozens of chichi restaurants, spas and hotels – such as elegant Il San Pietro di Positano and chic, intimate Le Sirenuse.

## Guam

This under-the-radar Micronesian island that's an unincorporated US territory is one of my favourite travel surprises. Before my partner and I first visited, I hadn't the faintest idea what to expect. But we soon discovered one of the friendliest – and most LGBTQ-embracing – tropical getaways in the Asian Pacific. Since Guam legalised same-sex marriage in 2015, it has also become a favourite wedding destination with queer folks from all over Asia and even Russia. We loved every minute of our visit, snorkelling in the bathtub-warm waters of Tumon Bay, hiking the emerald mountains of the island's interior, and eating great Thai, Japanese and local Chamorro food.

### Iguazú Falls

This natural wonder consisting of several waterfalls – the highest plunges 82 metres (269 feet) – is a dream wedding destination, and LGBTQ nuptials are legal in both Brazil and Argentina, the two nations that straddle this fabled stretch of the Iguazú River. There are plenty of photo-worthy lookouts for viewing the falls, but the most romantic way to see them is from a helicopter. For swish accommodation that also happily hosts same-sex weddings, consider the Belmond Hotel das Cataratas on the Brazil side and the Gran Meliá Iguazú in Argentina.

### Key West

Among famous LGBTQ resort towns, Key West has always stood out for its blissfully laid-back pace, unabashedly campy personality and remote location at literally the end of the road (it's closer to Cuba than it is to the US mainland). There are several gay-owned – and in some cases clothing-optional – guest houses, plus a slew of cushy mainstream hotels by the water. Do visit the Ernest Hemingway Home (and play with the friendly six-toed cats, descendants of Papa's original brood) and the small but interesting Tennessee Williams Museum. Other than that, I recommend that you divide your time between lying in a deck chair on a bougainvillea-choked lanai while sipping mojitos, and slurping raw oysters at a patio restaurant on funky Duval Street.

It's easy enough to escape for the day and hike amid the stunning canyons and desert peaks.

## Marfa

Rock Hudson, James Dean and Liz Taylor spent weeks in this high-desert ranching town in far West Texas filming the Hollywood epic *Giant* in the mid-1950s. Two decades later, the late minimalist artist Donald Judd transformed Marfa into a centre of contemporary art, fashion and photography. Potential sightings of the as-yet-unexplained 'Marfa Lights' on the horizon lend a touch of mystery, and a clutch of stylish eateries and cooler-than-thou hotels have helped vault this visually striking town into a favourite destination for LGBTQ weddings and romantic retreats. My only quibble is with the eye-roll-inducing hipster quotient, but it's easy enough to escape for the day and hike amid the stunning canyons and desert peaks of nearby Big Bend National Park.

## Paris

Although known less for its queer scene than Berlin or Amsterdam, the City of Lights is crazily romantic. Opportunities for magical moments abound, and you needn't feel self-conscious about doing touristy things – say, a leisurely arm-in-arm ramble along the left bank of the Seine to the Eiffel Tower, or a daytrip to marvel at the gilded quarters and fragrant gardens of Château de Versailles. But also visit the slender lanes and redbrick houses of the chicly bohemian Marais neighbourhood, with its adorable bistros, swank fashion emporia and low-key gay bars. And, at least once, wander without a map or a plan. Whether you're hoping to tap into the whimsical but sensual side of Paris that charmed you in *Amélie*, or the risqué, gay erotic side of the city that entranced you in *Paris 05:59: Théo & Hugo*, getting lost is the best way to create your own Paris memories.

## Provincetown

With a distinguished, queer-centric arts and literary scene and an idyllic setting at the tip of Cape Cod, America's original gay vacation town is beguiling for an amorous adventure. Saunter the length of colourful Commercial Street, popping in and out of festive bars, campy gift shops and respected art galleries. Sun your buns at clothing-optional Herring Cove Beach. Stay in a cosy and historic LGBTQ-owned inn. Or exchange vows in the gayest town in the first US state to legalise same-sex marriage. Do think carefully about when you go: July and August are wildly fun but crowded. The lovely spring and fall seasons see fewer visitors and, for lovebirds seeking solitude, winter is a delight.

## Port Douglas

This charming former goldmining port near Cairns is one of Australia's favorite queer beach hideways, offering direct access both to the Great Barrier Reef and the lushly tropical Daintree Rainforest. Check out the video of Kylie Minogue's bubblegum-pop hit 'It's No Secret' for a look at Port Douglas's gorgeous scenery (and some amazing late '80s hair and fashion). The pre-eminent LGBTQ venue is the Turtle Cove Beach Resort, a private 30-room clothing-optional resort overlooking a stunning crescent of sand. The Pink Flamingo Resort is another great gay-owned option, and you'll find dozens of other welcoming hideaways, many overlooking the Coral Sea and famous Four Mile Beach.

## Québec City

With its fairytale setting atop a cliff overlooking the St Lawrence River, the walled, 400-year-old Vieux-Québec district of this sophisticated city exudes old-world majesty. It's easy to feel instantly transported to Europe the minute you get here. Teeming with galleries and antiques shops, cobblestone lanes, sidewalk cafes and historic inns, it's a captivating place to steal away for a few days with your partner. For a modern break from the exceeding quaintness, it's a short walk to the youthful and buzzy Saint-Roch district.

## San Juan

If you want to marry or honeymoon in a tropical paradise with cosmopolitan elements, Puerto Rico's bustling 500-year-old capital fits the bill perfectly. San Juan has a welcoming LGBTQ scene, alluring beach resorts and the great charm of Old San Juan, a hilly warren of cobblestone lanes and colourfully painted buildings. Visit the 16th-century fortresses, Castillo San Felipe del Morro and Castillo de San Cristóbal, and the fascinating Museo de Arte e Historia de San Juan, which is set in a Spanish Colonial market hall. Many of the best hotels are along the oceanfront in nearby Condado, which also has a popular gay beach.

# Saying 'I do'

So you've decided to plan a destination wedding.
Congratulations! Combining your nuptials with your
vacation makes sense for all kinds of reasons: you
can choose the setting of your dreams and start your
honeymoon immediately. Tying the knot far from home
also eliminates the potential social obligation of having
to invite weird co-workers … or your homophobic
Uncle Frank. And there's the money you can save: a
12-person wedding at a posh resort can cost less than
a 120-person wedding in a drab ballroom back home.

Whether you seek a simple elopement or a grand gala,
here are a few tips on planning.

.

## Check the local laws

As of writing, all or parts of 30 nations had legalised same-sex marriages. Others – such as Japan, Cuba and Thailand – had taken steps in this direction. In some countries, same-sex weddings can be performed but won't be legally recognised. In other words, it's complicated. Know before you go. The good news is that new countries are legalising marriage equality every year.

## Figure out a budget

Place the word 'wedding' before any good or service – dress, cake, ring, corsage, balloon artist – and the price skyrockets. Shop around to find out what things will cost, make a list of features you want at your wedding, and decide what you're willing to spend on the whole event (don't forget travel costs). Most of your wedding expenses will go towards the site rental and food and drink, so start there.

## Work as a team

Sit down as a couple and talk openly about how you envision your wedding. You don't want to find out weeks into planning a *Mamma Mia*–themed reception on a private Greek island that all your partner wanted was a low-key barbecue in the backyard.

## Choose your date

A range of dates is actually the best strategy if you're considering a popular venue. Also think about seasonal pros and cons, like that a wedding at a ski resort is cheaper in late spring after the snow melts – but that melting snow probably means mud and black flies.

## Hire a wedding planner

Especially for large weddings, the planning process can be a lot to handle. There's choosing the right venue, booking hotel-room blocks, tailoring your outfits, and hiring caterers, photographers, DJs, florists and so on. An experienced planner, ideally one who has worked with same-sex couples, can save you hours of time and lots of stress.

Very early in my career as a travel writer, I spent several weeks in the Caribbean covering the cruise industry for a major guidebook publisher. I had a miserable time. Single, travelling solo and in my early 20s, I sailed one route after another, rarely encountering other people my age, or gay people of any age – many ports of call were conservative islands that to this day scorn the LGBTQ community. After about the 50th evening of making small talk with kind, elderly straight couples whom I'd randomly been assigned to dine with, I fled back to the mainland, determined never to set foot on a cruise ship again.

A few years later, a friend persuaded me to join him on a gay cruise. This time, *everything* was different. I laughed, I danced, I mingled, I had sex, I visited Mayan ruins near Cozumel and snorkelled in Key West. Cruise vacations aren't for everyone, and I still prefer the freedom of journeying independently on land. But I get it: cruises can be a blast. It's all about the company. It doesn't have to be a gay cruise – I had a fantastic time cruising through Alaska with my family a few years ago. But if you're going to spend a week floating around in a massive metal container, be sure to choose fun travelling companions.

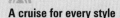

## A cruise for every style

Gay cruises can appeal to many interests: museum hopper or nature lover, beach bum or city goer, spa aficionado or shopping diva, singles looking to party or couples seeking relaxation. Some companies specialise in cruises exclusively for gay men or lesbians, others are queer-oriented but hetero-friendly. Some cruises offer a nonstop menu of pool parties, costume galas and cabaret and stand-up comedy shows. Others are mellower or more focused on ports of call than shipboard experiences. Just about any cruise can be incredibly romantic, especially if you score a cabin with a balcony, where you and your hon can snuggle together under the moonlight.

*Just about any cruise can be incredibly romantic.*

## Go with the pros

I have gay friends who will only sail on exclusively chartered LGBTQ cruises, and others who are just as happy on mainstream cruises, especially given that many of the world's largest cruise lines cater enthusiastically to gay travellers. Some standouts are **Azamara**, **Crystal**, **Holland America**, **Norwegian**, **Princess**, **Viking River Cruises** and the world's largest cruise company, **Royal Caribbean** (along with its subsidiaries, **Celebrity** and **Silversea**).

Among LGBTQ charter tour operators, good ones that offer several trips per year include male-oriented **Atlantis Events** (a favourite if you love to party) and **RSVP Vacations**, and lesbian-oriented **Olivia**. **R Family Vacations** has both adults-only and family-minded trips – they've been especially popular with lesbian, gay and transgender parents – while **Vacaya** welcomes guests across the LGBTQ spectrum and positions itself as less party-driven and more bespoke. **Brand g Vacations** specialises in more intimate trips, such as river cruises with less-common itineraries (the Scottish coast and Central America, for example). And boutique-y **Source Events** emphasises luxury – Tahiti and the Dalmatian Coast are a couple of its recent itineraries.

The cruise industry was hammered by the pandemic but has responded with ambitious new protocols – improved air-purification systems, more frequent cleaning, passenger health screenings and elimination of self-serve buffets (where these still exist, shipboard staff now serve the food).

## Find your ideal idyll

You can find gay cruises to all of the LGBTQ-friendly world's coastal regions. The most popular routes include:

- **the Mediterranean** (Lisbon, Barcelona, Rome, Athens, Greek islands, Tel Aviv)

- **European rivers** (the Danube, Loire, Elbe, Douro, Rhine, Seine and Rhône)

- **the Caribbean** (San Juan, St Barts, St Martin, Curaçao, Aruba, Cozumel and Key West; usually departing from Miami or Fort Lauderdale)

- **Mexican Riviera** (Cabo San Lucas, Mazatlán and Puerto Vallarta; usually departing from San Diego or Los Angeles)

- **Alaska** (Juneau, Skagway, Seward and Glacier Bay National Park; usually departing from Seattle or Vancouver).

Some other great ones that appear less frequently on LGBTQ itineraries include **Costa Rica** and the **Panama Canal**, **Antarctica**, **Hawaii**, **New England** and **Maritime Canada**, **Australia** and **New Zealand**, **Thailand**, and **Vietnam** and **Cambodia**.

# Finding romance

.

There was a time, not so terribly long ago, when if you were hoping to find someone special — whether 'bring home to mum' special or 'bring home for an hour or two' special — you hit the gay clubs and talked to people in person. Flirting IRL still happens, but these days mingling is done mostly on smartphone apps. And while technology makes it potentially easy to meet other queer people anywhere in the world, there are still certain places you should put at the top of your travel list if seeking a romantic connection on vacation.

Whether or not you're a fan of dating apps, the ritualistic nature of nightlife in many queer holiday destinations makes bar-going a viable way to meet friends – the daily 'tea party' at the Boatslip in Provincetown and the walkable clusters of lively gay bars in resort towns like Puerto Vallarta, Sitges and Wilton Manors (near Fort Lauderdale) spring to mind. Even at gay bars in less touristy places, it's the fresh faces from out of town who receive the most attention. Additionally, organised LGBTQ gatherings – cruises and group tours, ski weeks, circuit parties, Pride festivals – present plenty of great opportunities to mingle and make new friends.

As far as casual sexual encounters go, queer women and men continue to meet out at clubs and hook-up-oriented parties – the presence of go-go dancers portends a flirty vibe. And gay men still regularly meet and greet, shall we say, at queer beaches, in cruisey parks and at saunas and bathhouses, although the latter venues – actual commercial businesses that exist primarily to foster hook-ups – are on the wane, as they're generally less popular with millennials and Gen Z-ers.

## CAN I BUY YOU A DRINK?

Although there are far fewer exclusively gay (and especially lesbian) nightspots today than there were 20 years ago, queer bars are still great for dancing, drinking and socialising. They often function as de facto community centres that provide an easy way to tap into the local queer community. And most of the LGBTQ bars and clubs that are still going strong today – despite challenging economic times and competition from apps – have succeeded by adapting and improving their offerings, from higher-quality food and booze to better interior designs and attractive rooftop bars and back patios.

Not only are gay bars here to stay, many of them are more fun than ever. And if you're in the mood to dance, flirt, sing karaoke, and watch go-go dancers and drag shows (or maybe reruns of *RuPaul's Drag Race* or *The L Word*), there's really nothing like a club packed with happy queer revellers. (*See* p. 38 for a gay-bar crawl through New York City's West Village and its historic queer bars.)

Queer women and men continue to meet out at clubs and hook-up-oriented parties.

## SWIPING RIGHT

The great advantage of using apps to find fun on the road is that user profiles allow us to describe what we're seeking with far more finesse than if we're shouting over the din of Lady Gaga in a nightclub. Whatever your bag – you're in an open relationship, you're a couple seeking other couples, you're looking to fulfil certain kinks or fantasies – an online vacation encounter can offer you the chance to try new experiences far from home, where you're unlikely to bump into your boss or your neighbour on Her or Grindr.

Dating apps may ostensibly be for romantic liaisons, but they're also a great way to make friends – with or without benefits. My partner and I have used apps to find friends to hike with, to ask for restaurant recommendations and sometimes simply for a local perspective. We've made lasting friendships this way.

Here are some of the best apps around:

**Butterfly** – transgender-oriented, and with lots of safety and community-supportive features

**Chappy** – owned by Bumble and especially popular in the UK

**DaddyHunt** – geared towards older (however you wish to define that) men and their admirers in an environment free of ageism

**Fem** – lesbian dating app in which most users upload video profiles of themselves

**Grindr** – universally popular app for cis and trans guys seeking casual fun

**Growlr** – the favourite of bears

**Her** – great for lesbian, bisexual and queer women seeking friends and more

**Hornet** – geared towards casual hook-ups, and most popular with under-30 and Latin American users

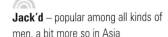

**Jack'd** – popular among all kinds of men, a bit more so in Asia

**OkCupid** – part of the massive Match Group network, and with a growing following among LGBTQ folks who identify in all different ways, including trans and non-binary

**Scissr** – particularly popular among women seeking casual fun with other women

**Scruff** – resonates especially with otters, bears and men in their 30s and older

**Taimi** – terrific all-round app because it verifies user identities and also partners with non-profits, such as the Trevor Project, that aim to fight homophobia

**Tinder** – somewhat more hook-up-oriented than its sister app, OkCupid, and popular with cis and trans queer folks of all stripes.

# Drunk gay
# history

λ

Many queer bars have been going strong for
generations – they're like living, breathing windows into
the history of the LGBTQ rights movement. **New York
City**'s **West Village** is the ultimate neighbourhood for
a historical gay-bar crawl. This isn't the city's trendiest
gay village – Chelsea, the East Village and Hells Kitchen
have more cachet these days. But there's something
endearing about hanging out in these unpretentious,
historic and very inclusive nightspots that have been
around for decades.

.

Start your adventure at the famed **Stonewall Inn**, which was designated a US national monument in 2016 for its role as the site of the 1969 Stonewall Riots. The original Stonewall Inn closed shortly after the riots, but the current incarnation opened in 1991 and remains popular.

Next, drop by **Julius' Bar**, one of the world's most storied gay establishments. It has been a tavern since 1864, was a speakeasy during Prohibition in the 1920s and began drawing a gay clientele in the 1950s. Scenes from the LGBTQ-themed movies *Boys in the Band*, *Love is Strange* and *Can You Ever Forgive Me?* were filmed here, and Tennessee Williams and Truman Capote were regulars.

A couple of blocks away, **Marie's Crisis** allegedly served as a brothel in the 1850s, and gained a discreet following among gay men in the 1890s – it also occupies the site where Thomas Paine, author of *Common Sense*, died in 1809. This cosy basement space is now a beloved piano bar and singalong venue catering to gay people and theatre lovers – it's not uncommon for established Broadway stars to pop in and belt out a few tunes.

Other LGBTQ hangouts in the West Village that have thrived for decades include **Ty's** (1972), **The Monster** (1981), the lesbian bar **Henrietta Hudson** (1991) and the **Duplex Cabaret**, which dates back to 1951 but has been in its current location since the mid-1980s – you may recognise it as the favourite performance venue of Jack McFarland on TV's *Will & Grace*.

Beyond New York, these legendary bars have long been fixtures in the LGBTQ community:

- **Atlantic House**, Provincetown (1798, and as a gay bar since at least the early 1950s)
- **Boate La Cueva**, Rio de Janeiro (1964)
- **Cafe Lafitte in Exile**, New Orleans (1933)
- **Café 't Mandje**, Amsterdam (1927)
- **Centralhjørnet**, Copenhagen (1917)
- **Finalmente Club**, Lisbon (1976)
- **Gay 90's**, Minneapolis (1920s)
- **Hula's**, Honolulu (1974)
- **Jacques' Cabaret**, Boston (1938)
- **Jeffery Pub**, Chicago (1960s)
- **New Sazae**, Tokyo (1966)
- **Royal Vauxhall Tavern**, London (1862, and as a gay bar since the 1940s)
- **Tavern on Camac**, Philadelphia (1920s, under different names but as a gay bar)
- **White Horse Bar**, Oakland, California (at least 1933)
- **Wild Side West**, San Francisco (1962, it's one of the world's longest-running lesbian-owned bars).

For many reasons – from having a sizeable student population to fostering sex-positive attitudes – these cities and resorts are ideal for romance on the road.

## Berlin

A trendsetter when it comes to art, fashion, dining and gender-queer, kink-friendly culture, Berlin rivals any European city as a top LGBTQ destination. Host of the continent's definitive leather and BDSM queer street-fair, Folsom Europe (the counterpart to San Francisco's Folsom Street Fair), it's home to an impressively diverse array of gay bars, fetish and underground events, and lesbian parties (such as L-tunes and Girlstown). The Nollendorfplatz area of Schöneberg has the greatest concentration of gay nightlife, but the city's queer scene permeates Kreuzberg, Prenzlauer Berg, Friedrichshain and Mitte, too. And Tiergarten Park – especially the wooded area south-west of the Siegessäule – is a free-spirited, clothing-optional gay outdoor playground.

## Chicago

The third-largest city in the United States is an alluring LGBTQ destination, and its wealth of attitude-free gay bars – most in the walkable Boystown district near Lake Michigan – makes it easy to meet people. Boystown is a 20-minute drive north of the city centre, with its iconic skyline of stately architectural gems and prestigious museums. The range of great spots to socialise – not only cool bars but artisan coffeehouses, trendy restaurants and fashionable boutiques – includes funkier and more lesbian-centric Andersonville to the north, and hipster havens like Bucktown, Logan Square and Wicker Park to the south-west. In summer, you can meet other queer folk at Kathy Osterman Beach, just north of Boystown.

## Dallas

Although catering more to business than leisure travellers, the 'Big D' stands out for its vibrant gay district, Oak Lawn, where you'll find about 20 LGBTQ bars (including one of the country's few remaining lesbian bars, Sue Ellen's), many with inviting patios and decks. And Dallas has lots of cool places to take a date, from the superb museums and performance halls downtown to its legit food scene. I had trouble deciding which of the five biggest cities in Texas to include on this list, as they're all fantastic for queer singles. Fort Worth has an underrated gay scene and a clutch of superb art museums. Houston rivals Dallas in its sheer variety of gay bars and is another hub of stellar arts and dining. And then there's all the fun to be had in Austin and San Antonio.

## Fire Island

The premier summer playground of LGBTQ New Yorkers since the 1940s, this narrow barrier island is reached by spending what might be the cruisiest 30 minutes of your life on a ferry boat – I've seen complete strangers at the start of this ride disembark as lovers. The gay scene is spread among two communities, the Pines and Cherry Grove, which are connected by a swath of sand and forest playfully known as 'the Meat Rack' and frequented by lusty gay men and – sometimes to the surprise of the former – dozens of very tame and curious white-tailed deer. In these unique villages, narrow wooden boardwalks are the 'streets' (cars are not permitted). There are a few hotels and a good selection of house rentals (Cherry Grove is generally more popular with queer women, the Pines more with gay men) – but book early as they're often snapped up quickly. Although Fire Island is a great place for simply chilling on the beach, the heady party scene runs at full throttle all summer.

## Fort Lauderdale

In the early 1990s, this breezy beach city in south-eastern Florida morphed into one of the world's foremost gay vacation spots thanks to forward-thinking gay entrepreneur Richard Gray. Clothing-optional men's resorts opened within blocks of the sugary-sand beachfront on the Atlantic Ocean, and dozens of lesbian and gay bars popped up both in Fort Lauderdale and adjacent Wilton Manors. Before long, Fort Lauderdale had surpassed Key West and nearby Miami as a world-class LGBTQ resort.

*The decadent vibe reaches a crescendo during summer, but Ibiza is a good bet year-round*

## Ibiza

The third-largest of Spain's Balearic Islands, Ibiza lies 150 kilometres (93 miles) east of Valencia in the Mediterranean Sea and is one of the top party spots – gay or straight – in Europe, particularly among fans of EDM (electronic dance music). Top DJs fly in to host massive parties at a variety of LGBTQ-welcoming venues, mostly in the main Ibiza Town port overlooking Eivissa Harbour. The decadent vibe reaches a crescendo during summer, but Ibiza is a good bet year-round for meeting fellow clubbers.

## Manchester

England's second-largest metro area has become a fashionable shopping mecca with a swirl of impressive postmodern architecture. It's also home to one of the continent's most spirited gay villages, Canal Street, a warren of cool eateries and lively bars that was the setting for TV's *Queer As Folk*. Less pricey than London and known for its indie music scene and devotion to football, youthful Manchester has an unfussy, progressive personality and hosts one of Europe's top Pride festivals.

## Mykonos

Long a haven of jetsetters, partiers and gay vacationers, this hilly island in Greece's Cyclades archipelago is a great choice for beach lovers who enjoy clubbing and meeting people (nightlife is centered on the main town, Chora). But this gorgeous, rocky island of whitewashed buildings and windmills, cheerful seafood restaurants and sun-kissed beaches also offers plenty for travellers wanting a low-key retreat. After all, there's no rule that says you have to dance all night, or visit in August when 30,000 other queer people flock here for the XLSIOR Festival.

## Puerto Vallarta

It's hard to name an LGBTQ resort that has more going for it than this friendly and affordable city on the gorgeous Mexican Riviera. Just south of the historic Centro, bustling Zona Romantica abounds with trendy lesbian and gay hangouts, an always-packed gay sauna, convivial open-air restaurants, and inviting hotels and vacation rentals just steps from the beach. During the day, Playa Los Muertos – with its curving, modern pier and golden beaches lined with thatched umbrellas – is a veritable sea of gay bodies.

## Rio de Janeiro

This Brazilian city of more than ten million is one of the most celebrated gay beach destinations in the world. Huge numbers turn out for Gay Pride in early July and the city's festive carnival celebration in February and March. But Rio is a fascinating, exciting place to visit year-round, with a splendid natural setting, a tropical climate and a vivacious personality. The city hugs the Atlantic Ocean, its neighbourhoods strung among white-sand coves and rocky mountain peaks, the two most famous being Corcovado – topped with its Art Deco–style statue of Christ – and Sugarloaf. You're rarely far from a powdery beach abuzz with vendors hawking fresh coconut juice and tropical cocktails. The city's energetic LGBTQ scene, centred in the seaside Ipanema and Copacabana neighbourhoods, makes Rio a perfect spot to find your dream date.

The lush pathways and greenery of nearby Independence Park are famously cruisey.

## Tel Aviv

Although LGBTQ tolerance is greatly lacking in the Middle East, Israel — and especially the seaside city of Tel Aviv — is a notable exception. This dynamic city of 435,000 claims to have the world's highest per-capita queer population and is famed for its nonstop clubbing and wealth of both queer and lesbian-specific parties. Gay-favoured Hilton Beach juts out into the Mediterranean and is ideal for swimming or just sacking out in the sunshine alongside scores of bronzing bathers. The lush pathways and greenery of nearby Independence Park are famously cruisey. Further opportunities for socialising await at Gan Meir (Meir Park), home to a gorgeous LGBTQ community centre, which has art exhibits, drag shows, transgender networking socials and other engaging events. For a romantic date night, head to the ancient Jaffa port district or swanky Rothschild Boulevard, which both hum with exceptional restaurants.

# The great outdoors

If you've recently found yourself dusting
off old camp stoves and sleeping bags that
had been languishing in your garage, or
shopping for new hiking boots or stand-
up paddleboards, you're not alone.
The popularity of holidaying far from
the madding crowds, in secluded forest
cabins or oceanfront yurts, isn't just a
self-isolating response to the pandemic.
Travelling to experience wild and natural
landscapes has been soaring in popularity
for years. Fortunately, we live on a big
planet, with no shortage of alluring,
secluded natural scenery.

You may need nothing more than a small patch of sandy beach for a fulfilling vacation. And in many places, secluded beaches also provide the perfect milieu for sunbathing and frolicking au naturel. The world's most famous gay beaches range from centrally located and conspicuous – such as **Queen's Surf Beach** in Honolulu, **Hilton Beach** in Tel Aviv, and **Ipanema** in Rio de Janeiro – to harder-to-reach spots that are more likely to be clothing-optional and are often hard to get to (and more than a little cruisey). Some famous examples include **Baker Beach** in San Francisco, **Black's Beach** in San Diego and **Wreck Beach** in Vancouver.

More great gay beaches in towns or cities with plenty of LGBTQ appeal include:

**Brighton Beach**, Brighton, England

**Cupecoy**, Sint Maarten

**Dongtan Beach**, Pattaya, Thailand

**Elia Beach**, Mykonos, Greece (*see* p. 45)

**Hippie Hollow**, Austin, Texas, US

**Little Beach**, Maui, Hawaii, US (*see* p. 54)

**Oval Beach**, Saugatuck, Michigan, US

**Playa Delfines**, Cancún, Mexico

**Poodle Beach** (more men) and **North Shores** (more women), Rehoboth, Delaware, US

**Rooster Rock**, Portland, Oregon, US

**Will Rogers Beach**, Los Angeles, California, US (*see* p. 119)

**Zandvoort**, the Netherlands

**Zipolite**, Oaxaca, Mexico.

## WALKS IN THE WOODS

If gay ski weeks are perfect for social butterflies who love playing in the snow, hiking getaways are ideal for sun lovers seeking solitude.

Even short hikes provide a great way to add some vigour and variety to a vacation otherwise focused on poolside drinks and late-night bar-hopping. Many gay playgrounds are within an hour's drive of glorious hiking terrain. Consider Palm Springs and Joshua Tree National Park, Hong Kong and the Dragon's Back Trail, Denver and Rocky Mountain National Park, and Zurich and Lucerne and the countless trails in the Central Swiss Alps just a train ride away, from Rigi Rotstock to Crest Hike in Stoos. These shorter adventures don't require a lot of gear, although I never travel anywhere without a small backpack with a water reservoir, hiking boots (or at least sturdy all-purpose shoes) and a lightweight (ideally solar) power bank to charge a phone.

> Many gay playgrounds are within an hour's drive of glorious hiking terrain.

## SUMMER GLAMP

Is your dream holiday more about marshmallows by the campfire than nesting in a plushly kitted-out hotel room? Consider spending your next trip in a tent, camper or even the back of a car at a campground. Or if you lack the gear, know-how or desire to immerse yourself in a full camping experience, consider glamping as a way to experience the joys of sleeping under the stars without roughing it.

Many resorts and even some national and regional parks offer glamping accommodation, which can be canvas safari tents, airy A-frame cabins, fanciful treehouses or mobile tiny houses. At the more basic ones, you may need to bring bedding and share bathing facilities. But some glamping accommodation is downright luxurious, with outdoor soaking tubs, fire pits and bluetooth sound systems – in other words, like plushly kitted-out hotel rooms. The website **GlampingHub** is a good resource – the site works much like Airbnb and has more than 35,000 listings worldwide.

> .
> Consider glamping as a way to experience the joys of sleeping under the stars.
> .

### Costa Rica

The gay-friendliest country in Central America is also a pioneer in ecotourism and adventure travel. This mountainous, tropical country that's more than 50 per cent rainforest is where the now ubiquitous sport of ziplining – that is, allowing yourself to be handcuffed to a cable and propelled across a vast abyss – was invented. (It's actually a lot of fun!) Costa Rica is one of the greatest places I can think of for LGBTQ nature lovers. It offers plenty of options for every budget, from cheap bungalows up in the rugged highlands to – especially on the Guanacaste coast – posh spa resorts such as Four Seasons, Andaz and Casa Chameleon. Since Costa Rica legalised same-sex marriage in 2020, it has become a wonderful gay wedding and honeymoon destination, too.

The top gay beachcombing and hiking destination is the Pacific resort town of Quepos. The gay-popular beach at Manuel Antonio National Park is a stunner. You'll sometimes spy adorable sloths snoozing in the treetops above you and playful white-faced squirrel monkeys cavorting in the jungle behind the sand. Note that by 'playful' I mean they might steal your sunglasses and throw shit at you. But they really are pretty cute. This is one part of the world where the mountainous highlands – especially around La Fortuna – are every bit as spectacular as the beaches, so do try to spend time in both regions.

## The Four Corners

Named for the point at which the American states of Arizona, Utah, Colorado and New Mexico meet, this spectacular expanse of jagged red-rock canyons, sweeping high desert and pine-shaded mountains takes in more than a dozen breathtaking national parks – the Grand Canyon, Zion, Mesa Verde and Arches among them. This is a big area with tons to see but relatively little development outside of the cities of Albuquerque, Phoenix, Salt Lake and Denver, which all have lively gay scenes and big airports. There are also some cool smaller cities and towns with bohemian personalities and cushy places to stay, with the New Agey arts hubs of Santa Fe and Sedona leading the pack. But to truly avail yourself of this area's awe-inspiring grandeur, head towards the sparsely populated, glorious scenery that lies nearest to the confluence of these four states. If I were forced to choose one place to wake up every morning for the rest of my life, it might just be the View Hotel – every room faces Monument Valley's gigantic Mittens monoliths, a landscape you'll likely recognise from dozens of Hollywood classics, from *2001: A Space Odyssey* to *Forrest Gump*.

## Hawaii

This tropical, LGBTQ-inclusive archipelago 4000 kilometres (2500 miles) west of the US mainland is the ultimate gay wedding destination, but it's also ideal for anything from a luxe spa vacation on the beach to an adrenaline-fueled sea-kayaking tour. The only drawback is that it's expensive, but you can find deals, especially during the spring and fall shoulder seasons. Hawaii comprises six main inhabited islands, two of which, Lanai and Molokai, are small and lack much infrastructure. That said, Lanai has two Four Seasons properties so, if you can swing it, it's a plum spot for a splurge. Molokai, because it's absolutely stunning and receives few visitors, is my favourite Hawaiian island for simply chilling out and hiking, but it has very few frills.

In the tiniest of nutshells, here's a cheat sheet to Hawaii's four most popular islands.

**Oahu** is home to the state's largest city, Honolulu, and about 70 per cent of the population. It has, by far, the most pronounced gay nightlife scene, near the tourist hotels of Waikiki. For singles, budget travellers and extroverts, it has the greatest variety of options – including noteworthy art, food and cultural attractions. But it can feel crowded and over-developed.

Arguably the best all-round island for a full range of experiences, from remote upcountry hikes to great beaches for surfing and stand-up paddleboarding, diverse and dramatic **Maui** abounds with sophisticated resorts and restaurants, most of them along the sunny west coast. Definitely visit the 3055-metre-high (10,023-foot-high) dormant volcano, Haleakalā, and make the topsy-turvy all-day drive to the verdant village of Hana.

The island of **Hawaii** (aka 'the Big Island') is about twice the size of the other islands combined. It's home to swanky resorts on its eternally sunny western (Kohala) coastline, and it's where you can explore a very active volcano, Kīlauea, the centrepiece of Hawaii Volcanoes National Park. My favourite spot is Hawi Town, a small historic village on the north shore.

The best major island for nature lovers and seekers of solitude is **Kauai**, a relatively small but magnificently lush land of rainforests, towering seaside cliffs and secluded beaches. Hikers flock to Na Pali Coast State Park, just beyond the picturesque village of Hanalei, which has been the setting for such films as *South Pacific* and *Jurassic Park*. Less developed than other islands, Kauai still has some luxe resort areas, such as Poipu and Princeville.

# Gay ski weeks

More than two-dozen gay ski weeks take place annually, mostly in North America and Europe, but there are a few in the Southern Hemisphere, including New Zealand's **Winter Pride Queenstown**; **Gay Ski Week Australia** in Falls Creek, Victoria; and occasional one-off events in the Chilean and Argentinean Andes Mountains. In addition to skiing and snowboarding, these gatherings often include discounted ski-and-stay packages and a slew of optional activities — including plenty for non-skiers — from mimosa brunches and evening dine-arounds to apres-ski cocktails around cosy fireplaces to snowshoe romps and zipline tours.

The granddaddy of them all, Colorado's eight-day **Aspen Gay Ski Week** launched in 1977 and continues to draw big crowds to this unabashedly ritzy Rocky Mountain playground. **Telluride Gay Ski Week** is another popular one in Colorado. Here are four more events worth waxing your skis for.

•

## Elevation Mammoth, California

Held in a sunny resort town in the eastern Sierras, this four-day event has long been California's favourite, although smaller ones like **Big Bear Romp** outside Los Angeles and **Lake Tahoe Gay Ski Week** closer to San Francisco also have plenty to offer. The organisers also present **Elevation Utah** in the affluent Utah resort town of Park City, and **Elevation Tremblant** in Québec, north of Montréal.

## European Gay Ski Week, Les Arcs

Among the continent's best-attended – and most party-driven – gay ski weeks (there are others in Austria, Switzerland, Spain, Norway and elsewhere), this week-long gathering takes place at Les Arcs, in the historic French Alps region of Savoie.

## Whistler Winter Pride, British Columbia

This seven-day party 120 kilometres (75 miles) north of Vancouver in the Olympic ski town of Whistler is a full-on celebration of LGBTQ culture, and has more of a following with women as well as a wealth of activities for non-skiers.

## Winter Rendezvous, Stowe, Vermont

Eastern North America's top event happens in the quaint Vermont village of Stowe, which is where the Von Trapp family settled following their escape from Austria at the start of World War II (and, yes, you can expect a *Sound of Music* singalong or two).

I love big cities, and I love quiet little hamlets in the middle of nowhere.

I love big cities, and I love quiet little hamlets in the middle of nowhere. This is also true of my partner, and it perhaps best explains why our two home bases are Mexico City, a jumbo-size world capital with about 20 million inhabitants, and the rural lake town of Washington, New Hampshire, population 1106. Our appreciation for these extremes frequently informs our travel plans. For us, the ideal is spending half of our trip in a big, culturally rich city and the rest somewhere quiet and surrounded by nature.

This approach also works well if you and your partner or travelling companions have something of a city mouse–country mouse dynamic that makes it hard for you to agree on one single holiday destination. If this sounds familiar, consider these city–country combinations that'll make everybody happy.

### Bangkok and Khao Sam Roi Yot

Talk about contrast: the propulsive energy of Bangkok – with its lively street vendors and markets, tumultuous car traffic, bustling gay clubs and shimmering skyscrapers – is just a three-hour drive from utterly tranquil Khao Sam Roi Yot National Park. We learned about the latter when we visited Bangkok for a week and wanted to spend a peaceful weekend at the beach without having to deal with an airport (this ruled out gay-popular Phuket, which is a 90-minute flight) or throngs of people (which ruled out another LGBTQ hotspot, Pattaya, which is only a two-hour drive but suffers from overdevelopment).

With a little research, we found a lovely, affordable boutique hotel – the OYO 500 Cordelia – a short walk from the beach and a half-hour bike ride from the park (the owners lent us bikes), and off we went, encountering few other tourists. Our greatest cost was hiring someone to drive us to and from Bangkok, but the convenience was worth every penny. At the national park, we explored the small, ornate temple inside Phraya Nakhon Cave, hiked directly beneath dusky leaf monkeys gambolling in tree branches just inches above us, and relaxed on a quiet beach. We went to Thailand partly for the food, and Bangkok indeed lived up to our hopes for amazing eating, but we also enjoyed two fantastic – and cheap – dinners in Khao Sam Roi Yot.

## Brisbane and Byron Bay

Australia's quintessential laid-back surfer town, Byron Bay has long attracted artists, latter-day hippies, queer folks and other alternative spirits. It's perched on the edge of the sea, just a two-hour drive south from the excellent art museums, verdant parks, buzzy rooftop bars and friendly gay scene of subtropical river-city Brisbane, and Byron's mellow vibe feels a world away from the rampant high-rise development along the Gold Coast, 90 kilometres (55 miles) north. This walkable town that's popular with both backpackers and celebrities offers plenty of cheap and carefree bars and restaurants, but you'll find some posh boutique resorts, too. Outdoorsy types appreciate the opportunities for surfing (it's a great place to take lessons if you've never tried it), scuba-diving, sea-kayaking and whale-watching.

**Cape Town and the Cape Winelands**

The LGBTQ vacation capital of the African continent, Cape Town actually offers a city–country adventure without leaving town. But it's also a great base for daytripping along the coast or overnighting just inland to visit the acclaimed vineyards and swank country inns of the Winelands region. Within Cape Town, you'll want to check out the Iziko South African National Gallery, explore the V&A Waterfront and take an aerial cableway to the top of Table Mountain, the dramatic monolith that defines the city skyline. You can also take a ferry to Robben Island, where Nelson Mandela was jailed for 18 years (it's now a UNESCO World Heritage Site and museum).

Spend a day driving south through the chichi coastal towns of Camps Bay and Clifton, stopping to relax on the gay-popular nude beach at Sandy Bay, before continuing south to Boulders National Park, where you can walk on a boardwalk through a colony of 3000 absurdly adorable jackass penguins (they're named for the braying donkey-like noises they make). The spectacular drive leads south to the Cape of Good Hope Nature Preserve, which has good hiking, lofty peaks, sweeping beaches and more amazing wildlife (though do keep a distance from the often aggressive baboons). Finally, give yourself at least a weekend – or maybe four days if you're a bit of a wino like me – to tour the verdant, sunny Winelands region, which is just an hour from Cape Town and is dotted with engaging towns, the most scenic and sophisticated being Stellenbosch, Paarl and Franschhoek.

**Copenhagen and Møn**

In Denmark's famously progressive capital – which embraces the avant-garde yet cultivates a warm sense of humility and hospitality – you're always treated like a friend. This centre of cutting-edge home-furnishing and architectural design has a compact, handsomely preserved core that showcases more than eight centuries of history and one of the continent's most fun-loving gay scenes. Like most Scandinavian cities, it's also an easy base for outdoorsy adventures. Options abound both around Zealand, the Danish island Copenhagen is located on, and just across the Øresund strait in Malmö and southern Sweden. One favourite excursion is the 90-minute drive to Møn, a breezy Baltic island and UNESCO biosphere reserve known for its dramatic white cliffs as well as hiking, stand-up paddleboarding, mountain biking, sailing and countless other recreational endeavours. In the largest town on the island, Stege, you'll find endearing galleries, eateries and a couple of good museums.

## Seattle, Vancouver and Victoria, with Salt Spring Island and Orcas Island

This enchanting adventure entails visiting a pair of great gay meccas, Vancouver and Seattle, then taking ferry boats to historic Victoria and around two lush, mountainous archipelagos: British Columbia's Gulf Islands and Washington's San Juan Islands. Surrounded by snowcapped peaks and pristine bays, Vancouver and Seattle are LGBTQ-embracing bastions of liberal politics, outstanding farm-to-table dining and creative energy. They also offer lots of outdoorsy diversions, from boating in Seattle's Lake Union to biking and hiking around Vancouver's enormous Stanley Park.

Whale-watching, sea-kayaking and strolling along driftwood-strewn beaches are popular pastimes out among the islands. Orcas Island offers a bounty of romantic inns, hip shopping and dining in the town of Eastsound and heart-stirring mountain hikes. In the Gulf Islands, I recommend Salt Spring Island, with its similarly gorgeous trekking, easygoing personality and charming places to stay and eat. Plus, each September the island hosts one of Canada's best small-town Gay Prides. Connecting the archipelagos by ferry, Vancouver Island is anchored by charming Victoria, a repository of both urban charms and natural beauty, with fine museums, cool cafes and a sizeable gay scene.

# Culture vultures

.

From scoring tickets to hit musicals
and must-see museum exhibitions to
simply walking through a city with a
rich history or an edgy design scene,
there are countless ways to create a
culturally immersive vacation. And it's
easy to give your adventures a decidedly
queer spin, with more LGBTQ film
festivals, history exhibitions and art
shows than ever before.

You'll find noteworthy cultural attractions in every big city and quite a few small towns. But some places – Mexico City, Tokyo – truly rise above when it comes to experiencing the arts. Here are five standouts that have vibrant – if slightly underground in the case of Istanbul – gay scenes.

The imperial heart of the Byzantine and then Ottoman empires, this compelling metropolis of 15 million people straddles the Bosporus Strait. The predominantly Muslim nation of Turkey has a chequered reputation when it comes to LGBTQ rights, but Istanbul — along with the capital city of Ankara — has a sizeable gay community. LGBTQ visitors should exercise discretion and take care to stay at hotels that are known to be gay-friendly, but this diverse city with incredible museums and historic sites is a fantastic design, food and art destination. Most of the gay scene is on the city's European side in the central Beyoğlu district, around Taksim Square and the Cihangir quarter. Favourite experiences include partaking of the hammam spa ritual at a traditional venue and exploring the vast and colourful markets, such as the Grand Bazaar.

*Favourite experiences include partaking of the hammam spa ritual at a traditional venue.*

### Five must-sees

· Hagia Sophia

· Topkapı Palace

· Dolmabahçe Palace

· Istanbul Modern

· Istanbul Archaeological Museums

## MADRID

A world capital in every sense – politics, commerce, gastronomy, LGBTQ culture – Spain's largest city is also legendary for its superb art museums and stately performance halls. It's the nation's centre of just about every artistic discipline and the home to iconic gay film director Pedro Almodóvar. Close to the city centre, Chueca is one of Europe's most exuberant gay villages – it's packed with queer-favoured bars, eateries and clothiers. Festival Visibles, an LGBTQ arts festival, takes place here during Pride, and the neighbourhood has appeared in numerous movies, including the queer dark comedy *Chuecatown* and – most famously – Almodóvar's *Tie Me Up! Tie Me Down!*, which was shot in the late 1980s, when Chueca was a seedy precursor to its fashionable current self.

> Chueca is one of Europe's most exuberant gay villages.

### Five must-sees

- Prado National Museum
- Museo Nacional Thyssen-Bornemisza
- Museo Nacional Centro de Arte Reina Sofía
- Museo Sorolla
- Museo Lázaro Galdiano

## MEXICO CITY

Said to contain more museums than any city but London, this cultural focal point of Latin America appeals especially to devotees of art and archaeology. You could spend several days examining the incredible trove of artefacts in the Museo Nacional de Antropología, before touring the ruins preserved at Museo del Templo Mayor, next to the city's imposing cathedral, or making the 48-kilometre (30-mile) trip to climb the amazing Aztec pyramids at Teotihuacán. Despite the city's old-world ambience, it's also a pillar of modern and contemporary art. In the charmingly bohemian Spanish Colonial neighbourhood of Coyoacán and its affluent neighbour, San Ángel, you can tour the former homes of Frida Kahlo and Diego Rivera. Mexico City gets bonus points for its affordable museum admissions and, when you're not out museum-hopping, you can happily explore enchanting neighbourhoods like Roma, Condesa and Cuauhtémoc, which abound with trendy mezcal bars, queer-popular cafes and hipster restaurants.

### Five must-sees

· Museo Nacional de Antropología

· Palacio de Bellas Artes

· Museo Frida Kahlo

· Museo de Arte Popular

· Museo Universitario Arte Contemporáneo (MUAC)

The world's largest metropolitan area – with 37.4 million residents and counting – Tokyo is a land of superlatives. The city's inventive art and architecture offer the perfect antidote to anyone turned off by sombre neoclassical museums with staid, Eurocentric holdings. The Roppongi Hills district, with Tadao Ando's sleek 21_21 Design Sight and Kisho Kurokawa's curvilinear National Art Center, contains some of Asia's most exciting buildings, but also be sure to walk along Omotesando Avenue in Harajuku, a promenade of edgy fashion and cosplay couture (note Prada's weirdly wonderful concave-glass-panel showroom). In Tokyo you can also find museums devoted to digital art, origami, ramen, snow globes, love dolls, sewerage and parasites (the gift shop is *very* strange). Lined with colourful sex shops and several hundred (often tiny) gay bars, the narrow alleyways of the Shinjuku Ni-chōme aren't a museum per se, but they're fascinating to explore.

### Five must-sees

- Tokyo National Museum

- National Art Center

- Ghibli Museum

- Mori Art Museum

- Edo-Tokyo Museum

## WASHINGTON, DC

A bit saddled, as many world capitals are, with the dull hum of bureaucracy, Washington has one major saving grace: it's an incredible museum city. The Smithsonian Institute operates 17 free museums and galleries, most of them near the regal monuments of the Capitol Mall. As you delve deeper into this city that also offers a pretty lively queer scene, you'll find plenty of other gems, including the Phillips Collection, the International Spy Museum and the National Museum of Women in the Arts. And there's more close by, including the stunning Glenstone contemporary art museum in Maryland, and the many outstanding attractions of Baltimore – the home of renowned queer filmmaker John Waters – including the American Visionary Arts Museum.

·
Washington
has one major
saving grace: it's
an incredible
museum city.
·

### Five must-sees

· Smithsonian National Museum of Natural History

· National Museum of African American History and Culture

· National Gallery of Art

· United States Holocaust Memorial Museum

· National Air and Space Museum

# Queer museums

All different kinds of museums address LGBTQ culture in thoughtful, original ways, from presenting impressively curated history exhibitions to celebrating the legacies of queer artists such as Rosa Bonheur, Robert Mapplethorpe and Jasper Johns. The **Canadian Museum of History** in Gatineau, just across the river from Ottawa, has one of the world's better permanent exhibitions on LGBTQ history, and on the other side of the country, at British Columbia's University of Victoria, you can visit the encyclopaedic **Transgender Archives**. Holocaust museums and memorials also discuss queer people from a human rights perspective. Of particular note are the **Memorial to Homosexuals** persecuted under Nazism at the eastern edge of Tiergarten park in Berlin, across the street from the larger **Memorial to the Murdered Jews of Europe**, and the triangular **Homomonument** on Amsterdam's Keizersgracht canal, which is steps from the house of Anne Frank.

.

A growing number of museums are specifically devoted to LGBTQ heritage. Begun in 1969, New York City's **Leslie-Lohman Museum of Art** features more than 30,000 works and objects. And in Brooklyn's Park Slope, you can visit the extensive **Lesbian Herstory Archives**. Berlin's **Schwules Museum**, set in a spacious restored printing factory in the city's Mitte district, contains an incredible trove of documents and artefacts about LGBTQ history. Fort Lauderdale's **Stonewall National Museum & Archives** has the nation's largest LGBTQ lending library, and next door you can tour the moving **World AIDS Museum and Educational Center**.

Museums devoted to historical LGBTQ figures include:

- **Andy Warhol Museum**, Pittsburgh, US
- **Charles Demuth Museum**, Lancaster, US
- **Dorking Museum** (E.M. Forster), West Hackhurst, England
- **Emily Dickinson Home**, Amherst, US
- **Georgia O'Keeffe Museum** (as well as her studio in nearby Abiquiú), Santa Fe, US
- **Glass House** (Philip Johnson), New Canaan, US
- **Grant Wood Studio**, Cedar Rapids, US
- **Jean Cocteau Museum–Severin Wunderman Collection**, Menton, France
- **Leonardo da Vinci Museum**, Florence, Italy
- **Maison de Balzac**, Paris, France
- **Monk's House** (Virginia Woolf), East Sussex, England
- **Musée Rimbaud**, Charleville-Mézières, France
- **Museo Frida Kahlo**, Mexico City, Mexico
- **Newstead Abbey** (Lord Byron), Nottinghamshire, England
- **Oscar Wilde House**, Dublin, Ireland
- **President James Buchanan's Wheatland**, Lancaster, US
- **Tennessee Williams Museum**, Key West, US
- **Thomas Mann Museum**, Nida, Lithuania
- **Walt Whitman House**, Camden, US
- **Wilfred Owen Museum**, Birkenhead, England.

As much as any art form, film resonates deeply with the LGBTQ community. Homosexuality has been depicted on film for more than a century, from Charlie Chaplin's *Behind the Screen* in 1916 to increasingly more explicit depictions from the 1960s to the present day, with critical hits like *Call Me by Your Name*, *The Favourite* and *Milk* earning best pictures nominations in the Academy Awards, and *Moonlight* winning in this category in 2017.

Since San Francisco's still outstanding **Frameline Film Festival** debuted in 1977, queer film festivals have boomed in popularity, and the city is also home to the superb **San Francisco Transgender Film Festival**. Other prestigious LGBTQ fests include **OutFest** in Los Angeles, **BFI Flare** in London, **Inside Out** in Toronto, **OUTshine** in Miami and Fort Lauderdale, the **Melbourne Queer Film Festival**, **Reeling** in Chicago, **Fire!!** in Barcelona, and **Queer Screen**, which is part of Sydney Mardi Gras. Some less obvious places with increasingly respected queer film festivals include Durban, South Africa; Long Beach and Durham, US; and Lisbon, Portugal. There's also **QDoc** in Portland, Oregon, the world's top showcase for queer documentary filmmaking, and **Lesflicks**, the lesbian film showcase at LFEST in Wales.

Here are three more great ones held in cities that also offer plenty of other reasons to visit.

### GAZE Dublin

Ireland's literary, cultural, political and LGBTQ capital hosts this outstanding queer film showcase presented by the Irish Film Institute. Formed in 1992, it's the largest LGBTQ event in Ireland after Dublin Pride. This progressive and welcoming city where the River Liffey empties into the Irish Sea offers plenty of reasons to stick around after the festival, from enjoying the friendly gay hangouts of the Temple Bar district to catching a play at an acclaimed theatre to walking by the Oscar Wilde statue in lovely Merrion Square.

**KASHISH Mumbai International Queer Film Festival**

Few countries have made greater progress lately with LGBTQ rights than India. Although it still has a long way to go, India decriminalised homosexuality in 2018, and highly visible queer communities have emerged in Delhi, Goa, Bangalore and especially Mumbai, the country's gay epicentre. An excellent time to experience this exciting coastal city of elegant hotels and restaurants, fascinating street markets and the incomparable Chhatrapati Shivaji Maharaj Vastu Sangrahalaya museum is during the KASHISH Mumbai International Queer Film Festival. Launched only in 2010, it has quickly earned a reputation as one of the world's top LGBTQ cinematic events.

**qFlix Philadelphia**

This week-long event does a great job nurturing young and emerging queer filmmakers from all around the world. It offers a great opportunity to visit vibrant and LGBTQ-welcoming Philadelphia, with its superb art museums and historic attractions, along with fantastic restaurants. Be sure to stroll around Independence National Historical Park and through Fairmount Park, with its groomed paths meandering along the Schuylkill River. And make the one-hour drive to the charming river town of New Hope, a relaxing gay weekend getaway with charming inns, colourful bars and cafes and the outstanding Bucks County Playhouse.

If you're a fan of the arts, the world's iconic performing arts venues – the **Sydney Opera House**, Vienna's **Staatsoper**, LA's **Walt Disney Concert Hall**, Beijing's **National Centre for the Performing Arts** – can be the highlight of a vacation. Try to buy tickets ahead of your visit, and look into booking a behind-the-scenes tour. Your perspective on Amsterdam's **Concertgebouw** or the **Teatro Colón** in Buenos Aires will never be the same after you've gazed out from the stage of one of these magnificent buildings.

For the ultimate arts vacation, consider attending a major festival.

For the ultimate arts vacation, consider attending a major festival. Although most of these suspended their in-person performances during the pandemic, the big ones are already coming back better than ever.

Shakespeare festivals are often a great choice, even if you're not fully onboard with works of the Bard himself, as some of the biggest – like the **Oregon Shakespeare Festival** in Ashland and the **Stratford Festival** in Ontario – present a mix of Shakespearean classics and modern plays and musicals.

If you're into experimental theatre – along with dance, comedy, cabaret and music – fringe festivals are an excellent way to go. The mother of all of these, **Edinburgh Festival Fringe** began in 1947 and is now the world's largest, held over nearly a month and featuring more than 3500 performances at some 300 venues. There's always an extensive slate of LGBTQ programming at these festivals. The UK has several other acclaimed fringe festivals, including a month-long showcase in the gay beach city of **Brighton**. Other top fringe festivals include **Adelaide** (the largest in the Southern Hemisphere), **Edmonton** (Canada's most prestigious) and **Orlando** (the oldest in the US).

Opera festivals are another favourite way to appreciate the arts in a memorable destination. Standouts include the **Arena di Verona Festival** in Italy, **Santa Fe Opera** in New Mexico, the **Salzburg Festival** in Austria, the **Glyndebourne Opera Festival** in England and the **Tanglewood Festival** in western Massachusetts.

# Pride and parties

.

Exactly 50 years after the advent of modern
Gay Pride celebrations, the tragic dawning of
the COVID-19 pandemic stopped most in-
person gatherings. Hopefully, by the time you're
reading this book, we'll all once again be able to
gather in groups – even if socially distanced – for
Pride festivals and other major LGBTQ events,
like circuit parties, queer film festivals (*see* p. 72)
and gay ski weeks (*see* p. 56). The pandemic
may have forced us to press pause, but Pride
marches *will* return. And once they do, these
empowering – and often wildly spirited – events
will continue to serve as a memorable focal
point for a fun-filled queer vacation.

On a humid June afternoon in 2016, my partner and I stood on a grassy median strip on Decatur Street in New Orleans's jubilant French Quarter and watched that city's annual Pride parade. We smiled as we cheered on the procession alongside a diverse mix of queer folks and allies, and more than a few tourists who'd probably never seen an LGBTQ Pride parade before. The colourful floats and teams of dancers across the gender spectrum passed by: Miss Gay New Orleans and her drag entourage, Elvis impersonators in pompadour wigs and tight leather shorts, the Big Easy Sisters of Perpetual Indulgence, Planned Parenthood volunteers and a riot of queer Mardi Gras krewes.

And then an empty float rolled by. I instantly felt a lump in my throat and tears welled up in my eyes. Along followed 49 marchers, each holding a placard with the name and picture of somebody who had been murdered just six days earlier in the Orlando Pulse nightclub shooting.

Attending a Pride parade can evoke an astounding range of emotions: unbridled hilarity, righteous anger, hopeful optimism and – sometimes – immense sorrow. For many of us, the overriding emotion is a feeling of spirited camaraderie. If you've never attended a Pride festival, or you've never travelled from home to be part of one somewhere else, I highly recommend doing so. Pride festivals are always a lot of fun, and sometimes they're downright transformative.

Virtually all of the destinations in this book host an annual Pride event. As exciting as it can feel to watch a massive Pride march in the heart of a big, LGBTQ-embracing metropolis like Los Angeles or Mexico City, it can feel every bit as inspiring to witness a gathering in a part of the world where the struggle for acceptance and human rights still faces enormous challenges. It could be in a deeply conservative little town like Starkville, Mississippi, which held its first Pride march in 2018, but only after fighting tirelessly to reverse an initial decision denying organisers a permit. Or it might be a parade in a city like Istanbul, Turkey, or St Petersburg, Russia, where authorities have banned Pride events and participants risk their lives to take a stand.

You may not wish to – and probably shouldn't, for your own safety – attend a Pride event someplace where doing so could get you arrested. But it's worth remembering, especially when you're happily dancing and partying throughout a Pride weekend some place where LGBTQ acceptance is now a given, that these gatherings began as courageously defiant political protests – and, in many parts of the world, they remain exactly that.

Where are the world's best Pride celebrations? The answer depends on what you're looking for. If it's a massive parade and festival with celebrity headliners and days of animated parties leading up to the big weekend, look to **New York City** (*see* p. 6), **Toronto** (*see* p. 12), **Madrid** (*see* p. 66), **São Paulo** (*see* p. 10), **Washington, DC** (*see* p. 69) and other major cities with similarly huge LGBTQ scenes. Increasingly, many places also hold trans Pride rallies, dyke Pride marches, and other events that speak to the diversity of the queer community.

Some of the most dynamic Pride festivals take place in less obvious cities. Baltic Pride – which rotates among **Riga**, **Latvia**; **Tallinn**, **Estonia**; and **Vilnius**, **Lithuania** – has rapidly become one of Europe's most spirited Pride events. Other cities in this part of the world that pack in a ton of exciting activities include **Brighton**, **Cologne**, **Palermo**, **Hamburg** and **Antwerp**.

In the US, impressive celebrations take place each year in **St Petersburg**, **Florida**; **Long Beach**, **California**; **Milwaukee**, **Wisconsin**; **Columbus**, **Ohio**; **Salt Lake City**, **Utah**; and **Charlotte**, **North Carolina**. Brazil is South America's top nation when it comes to Gay Pride, with the less touristy city of **Belo Horizonte** holding one of its largest festivals. **Cartagena** in Colombia hosts the biggest Gay Pride in the Caribbean, and the Pride march in **Manila**, in the Philippines, continues to mushroom in popularity.

# Travel and the transgender community

Although LGBTQ acceptance continues to grow around the world (broadly speaking), measuring progress can be complicated for transgender travellers. 'When travel locales are advertised to cisgender gay people, they tend to emphasise their own vibrant gay community,' says transgender advocate Gillian Branstetter. 'Transgender people tend to be a bit more concerned with other issues while travelling, including their safety, privacy and ability to go through airport security.'

Indeed, even LGBTQ-oriented businesses sometimes fall short in addressing the needs of trans travellers – it's not uncommon, for instance, for staff at gay bars to hassle or turn away trans patrons because the photos on their IDs don't closely match their current appearances. It's a particularly unjust irony, given that trans people of colour were among the most prominent forces behind the Stonewall riots.

Fortunately, there's an ever-growing number of annual gatherings organised by and for the trans community. Transgender film festivals take place annually in Amsterdam, Berlin, Kiel (Germany), Melbourne, San Francisco, Seattle, Stockholm, Sydney and Toronto, and Trans Marches are becoming a key feature of many Pride festivals, with some of the most prominent taking place in London, Paris, San Francisco, Toronto and Washington, DC. There are also several annual transgender events of note, including the Southern Comfort Transgender Conference (SOCO) in Fort Lauderdale, Sparkle Weekend in Manchester and the Koovagam Festival in the state of Tamil Nadu in India.

### Amsterdam Pride

There may not be a more distinctive procession than Amsterdam's Canal Pride in early August. During this vibrant celebration, the Pride floats are actually colourfully decorated boats, which glide along the city's famously picturesque canals. This is a great time to holiday in one of the world's LGBTQ capitals.

### Iceland Winter Pride

Begun in 2011, this three-day Pride in queer-positive Iceland is the wintertime counterpart to the more traditional (and still enormously fun) Reykjavík Pride festival in August. Held in early March, when temperatures hover around freezing, it's one of several Winter Prides around the world – some other notable ones, often tied in with gay ski weeks (*see* p. 56), are held in the outdoorsy Canadian resort towns of Whistler and Jasper, and in Queenstown, New Zealand. The Iceland event, known officially as Rainbow Reykjavík, features a mix of parties as well as tours to the Blue Lagoon and Thingvellir National Park and even a night-time Northern Lights excursion.

### Rhode Island Pride

Proof that big Pride celebrations sometimes come in small packages, this early June gathering in the vibrant little New England city of Providence typically draws more than 100,000 to watch one of the world's only illuminated night-time Pride parades. This charming, liberal city an hour south of Boston also stands out for its inspired food scene and youthful, creative vibe.

### Sydney Gay and Lesbian Mardi Gras

Begun in 1978, this three-week summer showcase of cultural events, parties and parades rivals any LGBTQ festival on the planet. And in Melbourne, Australia's other major queer hub, **Midsumma Festival** is a similarly fabulous three-week mix of Pride-related celebrations.

### Taiwan Pride

The largest 'in person' Pride to take place after the onset of the pandemic, Taiwan Pride drew more than 130,000 participants and spectators in 2020 – still well below the usual attendance of at least 200,000. Asia's largest Pride event is a reflection of Taiwan's reputation as the continent's leader in gay rights (in 2019 it became the first place in Asia to legalise same-sex marriage). Taiwan Pride is always held in autumn, which is my favourite time (the weather is mild and dry) to visit this friendly island and its largest city, Taipei. Be sure to investigate the city's lively gay nightlife district, centred around the Ximen Red House complex.

## GAY CIRCUIT PARTIES AND OTHER FESTIVALS

If you're a social butterfly with a passion for partying, consider planning your next vacation around one of the globe's many famous annual circuit party weekends. These events feature dusk-to-dawn (or longer) parties hosted by world-class DJs.

Circuit parties have long-held reputations for enthusiastic recreational drug use and for having a particularly avid following among men with chiselled gym bodies. Whether or not that's you, attending one can be a blast as long as you love great music and dancing. Some of them serve as fundraisers for worthy causes, such as the **Miami White Party** in November and **Montréal Black and Blue Festival** in October.

### The mother of all circuit party towns

In addition to rivalling Fort Lauderdale, Provincetown and Puerto Vallarta as a renowned gay resort getaway, California's **Palm Springs** is the ultimate circuit party destination, especially in early spring, when this hot spot in the desert – about a two-hour drive west of Los Angeles – hosts two insanely popular LGBTQ parties. First, there's **Club Skirts Dinah Shore Weekend**, which bills itself as the world's largest lesbian gathering. Then the **Palm Springs White Party** draws a massive contingent of gay men for a weekend of pool-side revelry.

Year-round, you'll find this small retro-chic city with fabulous mid-century modern architecture rife with cheeky (pun intended) clothing-optional resorts and lively gay bars. Yet as much as it's a party town, Palm Springs is also a romantic desert oasis surrounded by natural wonders, from the soaring San Jacinto Mountains, which you can access from town via the world's largest rotating aerial tramcars, to the spectacular desert wilderness of Joshua Tree National Park.

Palm Springs is also a romantic desert oasis surrounded by natural wonders.

## More LGBTQ circuit parties and festivals

Want to build a vacation around a circuit party or festival? Try these standouts:

- **Circuit Festival**, Barcelona, August
- **Folsom Europe**, Berlin, September
- **Folsom Street Fair**, San Francisco, September
- **G Circuit Songkran**, Bangkok, April
- **La Demence**, Brussels, held monthly throughout the year
- **LFEST**, Llandudno, Wales, July
- **Memorial Day Weekend**, Pensacola, Florida, May
- **One Magical Weekend**, Orlando, June
- **Prism**, Toronto, June
- **Ptown Lesbian Festival**, Provincetown, May
- **Southern Comfort Transgender Conference**, Fort Lauderdale, August
- **Southern Decadence**, New Orleans, August–September
- **Velvet Lesbian Festival**, Ibiza, October
- **Winter Party**, Miami, March
- **XLSIOR**, Mykonos, August.

# Carnival season

Although it's held roughly around the same season, Sydney's LGBTQ version of Mardi Gras isn't linked to the world's many other carnival events, which are, historically, tied to the Christian liturgical season of Lent. These other celebrations conclude the week of Mardi Gras (aka Fat Tuesday or Shrove Tuesday), the day before Ash Wednesday. Depending on the year, Mardi Gras Tuesday can fall anywhere between 3 February and 10 March – it's always 47 days before Easter.

It's kind of amazing, when you consider their religious – and especially Catholic – associations, but many of the world's top carnivals draw *huge* numbers of LGBTQ participants. The top two in queer popularity are **New Orleans Mardi Gras** and **Rio de Janeiro Carnival**, both of which feature numerous parades and parties over the course of several weeks, culminating in some truly bacchanalian revelry – including a wildly colourful gay costume ball in Rio – on Fat Tuesday.

Other carnival locales where you can happily fly your queer freak flag include **Tenerife**, the largest of Spain's Canary Islands; **Venice**, **Italy**; **Cologne**, **Germany**; **Nice**, **France**; **Basel**, **Switzerland**; **Salvador**, **Brazil**; **Mazatlán**, **Mexico**; and **Québec City**, **Canada**.

# On the road

.

Don't you find there's something
exhilarating about getting into a car
and turning onto a long, black ribbon
of asphalt and driving? What about the
joy of zooming along a remote coastal
road, or zigzagging over a narrow
mountain pass, without a specific plan?
For me, an epic road trip is one of the
most thrilling ways to explore some of
the world's more scenic places.

I'm not opposed to travelling with a strategy. It's often helpful to book some accommodation in advance and keep to a rough schedule. But I also recommend building in opportunities to slow down and explore any intriguing roadside sights that catch your eye – maybe a farm-stand overflowing with juicy raspberries and crisp apples, or perhaps some sexy eye-candy sunbathing at the base of a rushing waterfall.

My partner and I take at least three or four extended road trips each year, partly because it's a great way to cover a lot of interesting territory, but also because we both just love being in the car. We listen to podcasts about movies, politics, food and pop culture, along with our favourite Spotify playlists, and we often break things up with impromptu hikes and leisurely lunches. We try to drive when it's light out, to fully enjoy the scenery, and almost slavishly avoid limited-access highways. Sure, doing so sometimes adds hours to our journey. But for us that's a good thing: as the cliché goes, getting there is half the fun!

Whatever your road-tripping style, here are a few specific things to consider when planning your grand adventure.

## Watch for one-way rental fees

In many places, rental car companies impose steep surcharges if you return your car in a city other than where you rented it. This means you may save a bundle by planning a round-trip rather than a one-way road-trip vacation.

## Book some hotels in advance

It's a drag pulling into town after a long day on the road and finding there's not a vacant hotel room for miles. Especially in popular places in high season, it's best to make advance reservations. But when possible, leave your plans open some nights and just see where the road takes you.

Had we booked everything in advance over the past few years, we'd have never stumbled upon such memorable places as Carhenge, a Stonehenge-inspired arrangement of 39 vintage automobiles in the rural plains of western Nebraska, or Cenote Palomitas, an underground cavern in Mexico's Yucatán where we swam in a deep-blue pool beneath a natural ceiling of eerie-looking stalactites.

## Avoid big cities

Driving in cities usually means stressful traffic and hard-to-find – and sometimes super expensive – parking. If I want to see any large cities on a road trip, I usually visit them at the beginning or the end, before I've picked up or after I've dropped off my rental car. If you do visit a city in the middle of a road trip, park your car someplace fairly affordable (such as an airport carpark) and use public transport while you're in the city.

Leave your
plans open
some nights
and just see
where the road
takes you.

### Bring picnic supplies

For longer trips, we always pack a couple of bowls, spoons and forks, plus a corkscrew/bottle opener, a box of sealable sandwich bags, a travel-size bottle of dishwashing detergent and a soft-sided, insulated, thermal food carrier. These items make it easy for us to travel with basic groceries (mostly breakfast supplies, evening snacks and booze) and help us save time and money by eating some meals in our rooms or at the many scenic picnic spots we pass along the way. Be sure to book hotel rooms with fridges for your perishables.

### And don't forget

A few other things to take include a bluetooth car adapter in case your rental car doesn't have a stereo with bluetooth, portable chargers for your smartphones and laptops (we have one that can also jump-start car batteries), and an extra change of warm outerwear and hiking boots to keep in the car in anticipation of interesting excursions and dramatic changes in the weather.

Here are four of the most amazing road trips I've made, all in progressive parts of the world where LGBTQ folks are likely to receive a warm welcome. All of these routes also contain a ton of 'holy shit, we have to stop and take a picture' viewpoints. The distances given are approximate – they'll depend on how many fascinating little diversions you discover.

### Nova Scotia and Maine

**Distance:** 2200 kilometres (1370 miles), including two ferry crossings
**Start and end:** Halifax
**Possible overnights:** Baddeck, Sydney, Chéticamp, Pictou, Charlottetown, North Rustico, Saint John, Saint Stephen, Bar Harbor, Boothbay Harbor, Portland, Camden, Bar Harbor, Yarmouth and Lunenburg
**What you'll see:** Some of the most stunning coastal scenery on North America's Atlantic Coast, and countless clapboard seafood eateries serving fresh lobster, mussels and scallops.

Begin in Nova Scotia's friendly and walkable capital city of **Halifax**, with its captivating seafaring neighbourhoods and the most visible LGBTQ community in Maritime Canada. Next up, follow the scenic 298-kilometre (185-mile) Cabot Trail through the rugged and windswept island of **Cape Breton**, home to the cliffside trails (keep your eye out for moose!) of Cape Breton Highlands National Park and small towns like **Baddeck** and **Chéticamp**, filled with lobster shacks and galleries with locally made hooked rugs, pottery and wood carvings. From the coastal village of **Pictou**, take a short ferry to **Prince Edward Island** (PEI), Canada's smallest and most laid-back province – taking an afternoon to stroll among the lively restaurants and colourful gardens of the small capital city of **Charlottetown** – before heading down the coast of New Brunswick, where you can overnight in the historic port city of **Saint John** or the quaint boating enclave of **Saint Stephen**, before crossing the US border into Maine.

Make your way down Maine's breathtaking coast, stopping in **Bar Harbor** to explore the rocky peaks and carriage trails of Acadia National Park, and in **Camden** and **Boothbay Harbor** – all picturesque coastal towns with gay-friendly B&Bs and sophisticated restaurants. I recommend going at least as far as the small harbourside city of **Portland**, with its incredible culinary riches – from craft beer to hip seafood eateries – and making the short side-trip to **Ogunquit**, an LGBTQ-frequented beach town that kind of feels like a miniature Provincetown. Backtrack to Bar Harbor and take the 3.5-hour ferry across the glorious Bay of Fundy to **Yarmouth**, Nova Scotia, following the scenic south coast through quaint port towns such as **Barrington** and **Lunenburg** on your way back to Halifax.

•

Explore the rocky peaks and carriage trails of Acadia National Park.

•

## Sydney to the Blue Mountains and Hunter Valley

**Distance:** approximately 645 kilometres (400 miles)

**Start and end:** Sydney

**Possible overnights:** Katoomba, Kurrajong, Broke, Newcastle, Port Macquarie and Terrigal

**What you'll see:** Forested cliffs laced with hiking trails, the acclaimed cellar doors of Australia's oldest wine region, and a sunny and breezy swath of the New South Wales coast.

From Sydney, make the easy 90-minute drive to **Katoomba**, in the heart of the rugged Blue Mountains, a vast expanse of plateau escarpments, mountain peaks and striking sandstone geological formations, much of it contained within Blue Mountains National Park. I always seem to bump into plenty of fellow queer folks out this way, often out and about among the many enticing eateries and quirky shops. Katoomba and the nearby towns of **Wentworth Falls**, **Leura** and **Blackheath** offer access to dozens of hiking trails, some that run along the tops of sheer cliffs and others that plunge more than 180 metres (590 feet), via steep staircases, into sweeping valleys.

To get to the **Hunter Valley**, it's quickest to drive across the Darling Causeway and then turn east through the northern side of the Blue Mountains – stopping to saunter through the lovely pathways of the Blue Mountains Botanic Garden. Spend an optional night in the cute town of **Kurrajong**, before cutting north up twisting and turning Putty Road into the Hunter Valley, where you'll find more than 150 cellar doors offering exceptional wine. Romantic inns and farm-to-table restaurants proliferate, many of them in the towns of **Broke**, **Pokolbin** and **Wollombi**.

From the Hunter Valley, it's just an hour's drive east to the inviting seaside city of **Newcastle**, which is flanked by dramatic coastal bluffs and gorgeous beaches. Newcastle is a lively university city with breezy sidewalk cafes and a visible LGBTQ community – it's especially fun here during August Pride Month. You can potentially detour approximately 240 kilometres (150 miles) up the coast to **Port Macquarie** – an attractive, fast-growing beach town that's home to the renowned Koala Hospital and that also boasts an impressive food scene – or head south along the coast back towards Sydney, detouring via **Terrigal** for a bite to eat or a stroll along the Norfolk pine–lined Esplanade.

### Spain – a grand tour
**Distance:** 2575 kilometres (1600 miles)
**Start in:** Barcelona; **end in:** Malaga
**Possible overnights:** Sitges, Zaragoza, San Sebastián, Bilbao, Madrid, Toledo, Valencia, Benidorm, Alicante, Granada, Sevilla, Ronda, Marbella and Torremolinos
**What you'll see:** This zigzag trek across one of the world's undisputed gay vacation nations leads through iconic cities and sun-kissed beach resorts.

Start in north-eastern Spain's epicentre of food, architecture and art, **Barcelona**, and visit the adjacent LGBTQ beach community of **Sitges**. Then cut inland across the arid plains of Aragon through underrated **Zaragoza** – worth a stop for its impressive Caesaraugusta Forum archaeological museum – and then up through the Basque region to experience the incredible food of coastal **San Sebastián** and the famously curvaceous exterior of the Guggenheim Museum in the bustling city of **Bilbao**.

Drive south to one of the world's LGBTQ capitals, **Madrid**, a good place to ditch the car for two or three days, before heading east to coastal Valencia by way of the ancient Imperial City of **Toledo** and the small river town of **Cuenca**, famous for its 15th-century 'hanging houses'. The country's third-largest city, **Valencia** sits along the Mediterranean and has several notable attractions, the must-see being Santiago Calatrava's City of Arts and Sciences. The next leg of the trip, south along the Costa Blanca, is a little tricky: either you stop amid the unfortunately ugly canopy of modern high-rises looming over **Benidorm** in order to partake of this small resort town's fun gay clubbing, or you keep going to the coastal city of **Alicante**, which is more picturesque but mellower (though it does have a few fun queer bars).

The last leg of this trip cuts west and inland into southern Spain's gorgeous Andalusian countryside, with its Moorish architecture, fragrant gardens and lively – if also in some cases overly commercial – beaches. Spend a night or two soaking up the rich heritage of hilly **Granada** and touring the incomparable Alhambra Palace, before motoring west to the region's largest city, **Sevilla**, with its narrow lanes, orange tree–shaded plazas and mesmerising flamenco shows. Make your way south to Costa del Sol, stopping in tiny **Ronda** – an ancient Moorish town perched high atop dramatic cliffs – and then work your way east through monied **Marbella** to **Málaga**, a brightly revitalised Mediterranean port city with a beautifully restored Old Quarter. The nearby beach town of **Torremolinos** is another hot spot with gay tourists (especially Brits). Like Benidorm, it's a bit lacking in curb appeal, but it's a great place to hit the bars and meet people.

•

Spend a night or two soaking up the rich heritage of hilly Granada.

•

## California's Central Coast

**Distance:** 1200 kilometres (745 miles)
**Start and end:** San Francisco
**Possible overnights:** Santa Cruz, Carmel, Big Sur, Cambria, Santa Barbara, San Luis Obispo, Monterey, Saratoga and San Jose
**What you'll see:** The legendary sea cliffs of Big Sur, along with both affluent and quirky seaside towns with gorgeous beaches and sophisticated creature comforts, like stellar restaurants, swanky seaside hotels and acclaimed wineries.

From **San Francisco**, drive south along Highway 1 through picturesque Half Moon Bay and then along a string of beautiful, uncrowded beaches – some of them, like Bonny Doon and Laguna Creek, quite popular with naturalists and queer folks – to the colourful college and surfing town of **Santa Cruz**, with its old-school pier and amusement park. Continue around the bay to visit the astounding Monterey Bay Aquarium and on to the famously charming **Carmel-by-the-Sea** for its exceptional winery tasting rooms and utterly romantic restaurants. Continue through Big Sur, a roughly 145-kilometre (90-mile) stretch of virtually undeveloped coastline – save for a few posh boutique resorts. The road clings to sheer sea cliffs, crosses over about 30 historic bridges, and offers up dazzling views of the verdant Santa Lucia Mountains and the azure blue sea. It ends in tiny **San Simeon**, where you can tour the wildly opulent mountaintop estate Hearst Castle.

You'll soon pass through funky little oceanfront towns like **Cambria**, **Cayucos** and **Morro Bay**, before entering America's Riviera: coastal **Santa Barbara County**, with its blissful Mediterranean climate, Spanish Colonial architecture, buzz-worthy wine country and sweeping beaches set against a backdrop of craggy mountains. At this point, you can either turn back up the coast or continue another 160 kilometres (100 miles) south to **Los Angeles**.

The road clings to sheer sea cliffs, crosses over about 30 historic bridges, and offers up dazzling views.

To return to San Francisco, backtrack through Santa Barbara to **San Luis Obispo**, a pretty college town famous for its Thursday evening downtown farmers market, and take the inland US 101 route up to **Paso Robles** – another hub of amazing winemaking – back to Monterey Bay, detouring for a hike amid the volcanic peaks of Pinnacles National Park. Spend a final night in **San Jose**, which you may be surprised to learn has a larger population than nearby San Francisco – and a vibrant gay community, too.

# Queer road-trips at the movies

Looking for inspiration for your grand auto tour? You'll find plenty of it on film. In compiling this list, I went for queer films with colourful journeys, but there are many other wonderful candidates that lack travel but contain mesmerising scenery — think *Call Me by Your Name* (Lombardy, Italy), *Portrait of a Lady on Fire* (Brittany, France), *Summer of 85* (Normandy, France) and *Brokeback Mountain* (the Canadian Rockies around Alberta, standing in for Wyoming).

.

Some of the movies on this list have explicitly queer storylines. In others, the queerness is more subtext or suggested. But they all have a certain LGBTQ sensibility. So, grab your popcorn, sit back and enjoy the show:

- *All About My Mother* (1999) – filmed in Barcelona and Madrid

- *The Adventures of Priscilla, Queen of the Desert* (1994) – filmed in Alice Springs, Broken Hill, Coober Pedy, Sydney (Newtown) and elsewhere in Australia

- *Boys on the Side* (1995) – filmed in Tucson, Pittsburgh and New York City

- *Carol* (2015) – filmed in Cincinnati (standing in for 1950s New York City) and elsewhere around Ohio

- *Cloudburst* (2011) – filmed in Lunenburg, Halifax and elsewhere in Nova Scotia (sometimes standing in for coastal Maine)

- *C.R.A.Z.Y.* (2005) – filmed in Montréal as well as in Essaouira, Morocco

- *Happy Together* (1997) – filmed at Iguazú Falls, Tierra del Fuego, Buenos Aires and elsewhere in Argentina, as well as in Taipei

- *My Own Private Idaho* (1991) – filmed in Portland and Seattle as well as Rome

- *Supernova* (2020) – filmed in Keswick, in England's Lake District

- *Thelma & Louise* (1991) – filmed in Moab and elsewhere around Utah, and throughout southern California

- *To Wong Foo, Thanks for Everything! Julie Newmar* (1995) – filmed in Lincoln and Omaha, Nebraska; Atlanta, Georgia; northern New Jersey; New York City and the Hudson Valley; and Monument Valley, Utah

- *Transamerica* (2005) – filmed in Prescott and Scottsdale, Arizona as well as various towns in upstate New York

- *Y Tu Mamá También* (2001) – filmed in Mexico City as well as Huatulco, Puerto Escondido and other towns in Oaxaca, Mexico.

# Foodie adventures

·

In case it wasn't already clear from the
Instagram feeds of your food-obsessed
frenemies, there's never been a better
time to eat your way through a vacation.
Over the past two decades, even gay resort
towns with once notoriously uninspired
restaurant scenes — we're looking at
you, Palm Springs — have transformed
themselves into bona fide food
destinations. Scoring a table at a buzzy
bistro is just one kind of culinary thrill.
You could also spend a day wine-tasting
or an evening at a rousing night market.
The world is your oyster.

It's hard to say exactly why so many LGBTQ-centric neighbourhoods used to be food deserts. As recently as the 1990s, LA's West Hollywood, Sydney's Oxford Street and London's Soho were packed with scores of lively gay bars, but also dozens of mediocre restaurants.

Thankfully, times have changed. In part, this is because many LGBTQ neighbourhoods have become more integrated and eclectic, supporting a broader mix of businesses and catering to increasingly diverse crowds, foodies among them. There are also more restaurants run by celebrated, openly queer chefs than ever before – places like Gabrielle Hamilton's **Prune** in New York City, Mark Gaier and Clark Frasier's **M.C. Perkins Cove** in coastal Maine, Iliana Regan's **Elizabeth** in Chicago, and Yotam Ottolenghi's several trendy **Ottolenghi** restaurants in London.

## WITHOUT RESERVATIONS

If you plan to visit any super-famous restaurants, reserve well ahead. It's not uncommon for hallowed halls of gastronomy like **Pujol** in Mexico City, **Noma** in Copenhagen and **El Celler de Can Roca** in Spain's Girona to book up weeks or even months in advance. If you can't find an opening using online reservation services, call or email to get on a waiting list, and see if your hotel concierge staff can pull some strings. If you're hell-bent on getting into a place, be flexible – if all that's available are a couple of bar seats at midnight on a Tuesday, go for it.

On the other hand, there's a lot to be said for leaving things to chance. I might occasionally book a dinner on a trip in advance. But there's so much incredible food out there, and my partner and I have had countless wonderful experiences simply venturing out to a neighbourhood we've heard good things about and seeing what we find. Our favourite strategy is the progressive, or safari, dinner – a plate of oysters and a couple of glasses of Sauvignon Blanc at a sidewalk cafe, followed maybe with steak tartare or a shareable salad at a bistro a few doors away, then green curry around the corner at some cosy-looking Thai restaurant, and finally ice cream to go – eaten on a park bench under the moonlight. In a city with interesting people-watching and a diverse food scene, it's hard to go wrong with this approach.

Whatever your style, call restaurants before you arrive, even if just to confirm that they're open. Don't trust hours posted online. This has been especially true during the pandemic, as policies and hours can change from week to week.

## COOL CULINARY DESTINATIONS WITH FUN BUZZY GAY SCENES

### Austin, Texas, US
*Known for:* barbecue (especially pulled pork and brisket), craft cocktails, food trucks, Texas-size steaks, Mexican-influenced food (from Tex-Mex to sophisticated regional Mexican fare).

### Brighton, England
*Known for:* local and sustainable farm-to-table (and an especially celebrated vegetarian) scene, oyster bars, hip brunch spots, bars with talented mixologists (and drinks made with local, small-batch Brighton Gin), Indian food.

### Hanoi, Vietnam
*Known for:* jam-packed night markets, Vietnamese coffee, French bakeries (for both pastries and bánh mì sandwiches), bun cha (fatty pork grilled with rice vermicelli), street food in the Old Quarter.

### Kyoto, Japan
*Known for:* ramen and nishin soba noodles (topped with cooked herring), among the world's most Michelin stars per capita, izakayas, craft beer, Nishiki Market (for incredible food and culinary wares).

### Lima, Peru
*Known for:* ceviche, upscale Japanese-Peruvian fusion fare (known as 'Nikkei'), picarones (fried sweet-potato donuts with scented syrup), street food (especially anticuchos, which are grilled and marinated beef hearts on skewers), pisco sours.

### Lyon, France

*Known for:* wine from the nearby Rhône Valley and Burgundy, artisan cheeses and sausages, salade Lyonnaise, North African food, Restaurant Paul Bocuse.

### Melbourne, Australia

*Known for:* regionally sourced ingredients (from Yarra Valley and Mornington Peninsula wines to fresh produce and seafood), one of the oldest and most impressive Chinatowns outside of Asia, both upmarket and affordable Italian food (and to-die-for gelato), artisan coffee roasters, leisurely boozy brunches.

### Portland, Oregon, US

*Known for:* craft beer and coffee, Asian food (especially Thai and Japanese), relatively inexpensive farm-to-table restaurants (usually vegetarian-friendly), superb food-driven happy hours, food trucks (called 'carts' locally).

### Richmond (adjacent to Vancouver), Canada

*Known for:* Chinese food (Cantonese in particular), British Columbia ice wines and Rieslings, food courts filled with cheap and locally owned international eateries, the Richmond night market, local seafood (especially salmon, crab and spot prawns).

### San Sebastián, Spain

*Known for:* pintxos bars, lots and lots of Michelin-starred restaurants, sublimely fresh seafood (especially salt cod, whole-roasted hake and turbot, and lobster), light and bright Txakoli wines from the Basque country, gorgeous Belle Epoque restaurant architecture.

It's like
attending a
small Pride
festival, but with
amazing food.

Some of the most delicious and entertaining places for exploring are food markets. No, I don't mean garishly lit grocery stores with aisles of processed snack foods. I'm talking about the joy of strolling around a sun-dappled, open-air farmers market on a Saturday morning, popping ripe blueberries into your mouth. Or the exhilaration of making your way through a sultry night market devouring skewered fish balls, pork-blood cakes and stinky tofu. These experiences can connect us closely to the places we're visiting – and offer the chance to try local delicacies that you may never find back home.

### Farmers markets

What to buy at a farmers market if you're visiting from afar? I stock up on goods that travel well: chocolates, honeys, jams, relishes, marinades, pickled veggies and even local beer and spirits. But if you're staying somewhere with a kitchen or at least a fridge, buy peak-fresh peaches and heirloom tomatoes, local pies, cheeses, nuts and smoked fish to enjoy during your holiday.

Even if you don't buy anything more than a breakfast burrito or a bowl of ramen to eat while you're there, the joy of a farmers market is its festive vibe – locals and tourists happily milling about, eating, chatting, flirting. In cities like San Francisco and Sydney, it's like attending a small Pride festival, but with amazing food.

Beyond the farmers variety, any marketplace can be a treat. In one of London's most inclusive neighbourhoods, **Camden Market** features more than a thousand vendors, from artisans to food purveyors, alongside picturesque Regent Canal. Near where we live in Mexico City, we take house guests to **Bazaar Sábado**, in the historic San Ángel neighbourhood, to shop for Día de Muertos decorations, gorgeous pottery and small-batch mezcal. **San Telmo Market**, in the gayest neighbourhood of Buenos Aires, has not only some of the finest coffee vendors in the city but also incredible antiques.

## Food halls

Long a tradition in European cities – think **Harrods** in London, **Östermalm** in Stockholm and **Galleries Lafayette** in Paris – food halls have become quite the rage worldwide. They can feature anything from cheap pork buns and burgers to upscale eats from famous chefs. Some, like the **Ferry Building** in San Francisco, also have outdoor farmers markets one or two days a week. In North America there are dozens worth mentioning, but among the old-school stalwarts, **Reading Terminal** in Philadelphia, **West Side Market** in Cleveland, **Pikes Place** in Seattle and **St Lawrence Market** in Toronto are all standouts. Newer, trendier takes on this concept include **Oxbow Public Market** in Napa Valley, **Ponce City Market** in Atlanta, **St Roch Market** in New Orleans and **Liberty Public Market** in San Diego. In Australia, **Tramsheds** and **Barangaroo South** in Sydney and **Prahran Market** in Melbourne are favourites. Elsewhere around the world, check out **Arts on the Main** in Johannesburg, **Mathallen** in Oslo, **Markethal** in Rotterdam, **Time Out Market** in Lisbon and **Maxwell Road Hawker Centre** in Singapore.

## Night markets

These colourful assemblies of vendors hawking everything from spicy fried chicken to knock-off Prada bags have their origins in Asia, where they remain a beloved tradition. Good bets include **Huaxi Street Night Market** in Taipei, the **Old Quarter Market** in Hanoi and **Temple Street** in Hong Kong. The hipster-approved **Chang Chui Plane Night Market** in Bangkok is actually built around a giant airplane (be sure to climb the steps for cocktails in the cabin). But traditionalists also appreciate the city's **Rod Fai** night markets on Srinakarin Road and in the Ratchada district.

The popularity of these free-spirited evening gatherings continues to spread outside of Asia, and you'll find impressive ones in Melbourne at **Queen Victoria Market**, the Vancouver BC suburb of **Richmond**, the Queens, New York section of **Corona**, and in Chicago's international **Argyle** neighbourhood. And don't forget the famously festive Christmas Markets in European cities such as **Prague**, **Edinburgh** and **Berlin**, where you can nosh on sausages or raclette while enjoying mulled glühwein.

Picture the scene: you and a date, reclining in Adirondack chairs around a firepit on a slate patio, acres of vineyards spread out before you, a glass of dry rosé in hand. There are few more relaxing holiday activities than exploring the undulating hills of a picturesque wine region. This once rather exclusive pastime has become increasingly egalitarian, and winemaking hubs tend to be lovely food-forward places with romantic B&Bs, gourmet food artisans of every ilk and easy proximity to cities with strong LGBTQ interest. You'll find excellent winemaking regions in most countries, but here are some of my favourites.

The **Sonoma Valley**, just outside San Francisco, makes for a fantastic wine romp – there's even an annual LGBTQ wine gathering, **Out in the Vineyard**, held there each summer. Other gay-popular vino-centric regions include Oregon's **Willamette Valley**, Washington State's **Woodinville** and **Walla Walla**, New York State's **Finger Lakes** and **Eastern Long Island**, British Columbia's **Okanagan Valley**, northern France's **Champagne** and **Burgundy**, southern France's **Rhône Valley**, Italy's **Umbria** and **Tuscany**, Spain's **Catalonia**, South Africa's **Cape Winelands**, Argentina's **Mendoza**, New Zealand's **Marlborough**, and South Australia's **McLaren Vale**, **Adelaide Hills** and **Barossa Valley**.

You can find cool brewpubs all over the world and, if you identify as a queer beer geek, here are several places that you should put at the top of your list. In Europe, head to **Antwerp**, **Cologne**, **Bristol** and **Prague**. While in North America, hops hounds should check out **Asheville**, **Brooklyn**, **Denver**, **San Diego**, and both **Vancouver** and **Victoria** in British Columbia. You can include previously mentioned **Melbourne** and **Portland** on your list too.

# Spit or swallow?
# The ins and outs of wine tasting

Visiting a tasting room or cellar door for the first time can feel slightly intimidating. To make the most of a day of winery-hopping, follow these few simple guidelines.

Take your time, and don't squeeze in more than three or four wineries in a single day. Allow at least an hour at each winery, and pause for a moment to reflect after you try each wine. You don't have to speak in esoteric wine jargon or come up with weirdly specific tasting notes ('hints of candied yams and rendered ox fat'). Just have fun figuring out what you genuinely like.

.

If you have to decide between the two, choose a winery with an amazing setting over one with amazing wine. You're on vacation, after all, and, at the end of the day, you'll remember a dazzling view or gorgeous architecture more than what you drank. If all you want is amazing wine, you can go to a bottle shop.

Don't be a know-it-all. Your ability to name all six red grape varieties permitted in a Bordeaux blend might help you win at pub trivia, but showing off your extensive wine cred in a tasting room is obnoxious.

You're not obligated to buy anything. As long as you're polite, pay any tasting fees and perhaps leave a tip if the service warrants it, it's not rude to leave without purchasing any bottles. Stock up if you love what you've tasted, but also remember that wine – like that turquoise belt buckle you bought in Santa Fe and never wore again – is often best appreciated in its original setting. Besides, realistically, how many bottles can you safely smuggle home in a checked suitcase? (In my experience, the answer is eight – carefully swaddled in dirty laundry – but two or three is a safer number.)

Pack a picnic lunch or visit a winery that serves food (you can't go wrong with cheese and charcuterie). Whatever you do, keep hydrated and avoid guzzling too much wine on an empty stomach. Tumbling drunkenly out of the passenger seat of your rental car is hilarious only if you're on an episode of *Ab Fab*.

And that brings us back to the eternal question: Spit? Or swallow? If doing so brings you joy, and you're not driving, go ahead and swallow every last drop. But keep in mind that it's perfectly acceptable – and in fact encouraged – to spit out your wine, especially if you're tasting a lot of it in one day.

# Luxury getaways

The good news about luxury travel is that you don't have to be fabulously wealthy to go on a fancy vacation. The bad news is that, if you aren't fabulously wealthy, a fancy vacation may only be in reach once in a blue moon. Here's how to live it up a little on any budget.

For most of us mere mortals, perhaps the best way to think about luxury is to come up with occasional ways to treat yourself. It could be a two-week ski vacation in Aspen or a spa getaway on the French Riviera. Or maybe it's just splurging for great seats at a Broadway show or upgrading to first class on a flight to Bangkok. There are all kinds of pleasurable ways to pamper yourself, whatever you like to do.

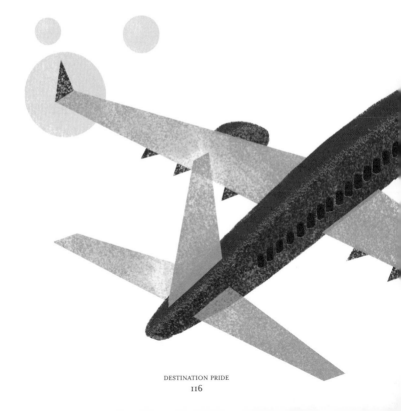

These days, virtually every major international hotel company is solid – and in some cases fantastic – when it comes to warmly welcoming its LGBTQ guests. Plenty of smaller exclusive hotel companies are also very LGBTQ-embracing, among them **Rosewood**, **Aman Resorts**, **Belmond**, **Red Carnation**, **Anantara**, **Mandarin Oriental**, **Montage** and **Langham**. And then there's stylish, gay-owned **Axel Hotels**, which has several properties in Spain and one each in Germany, Italy and the United States, and cheekily bills itself as 'hetero-friendly'.

If you really want to feel confident that you're in good hands, book your trip through an LGBTQ-oriented travel agency. Outfits like **Toto Tours**, **Olivia** (geared specifically toward queer women), **Zoom Vacations**, **Out Adventures** and **Out of Office** can plan every aspect of a luxury vacation and vouch for the inclusivity and integrity of all the companies they partner with.

> Plenty of smaller exclusive hotel companies are also very LGBTQ-embracing.

Most of the big cities I've discussed elsewhere in this book have plenty of swanky diversions and ritzy retail neighbourhoods to keep bon vivants happy – **Tokyo**, **London**, **Paris**, **New York City**, **Aspen** and **Whistler** stand out in particular. Here are seven more holiday spots where you can live it up like a royal.

## Bali

Although it's in Indonesia, a Muslim nation where negative LGBTQ attitudes prevail, the majority-Hindu island province of Bali is a creative centre of art, dance and music where same-sex couples can feel welcome – and there are dozens of blissful beach resorts with serene spas and idyllic ocean views. There's even a cool little gay nightlife quarter, Jalan Camplung Tanduk, in Seminyak, not far from sybaritic hideaways such as the Legian, Anantara and W Bali. Also check out the sands of Batu Belig Beach, where you're likely to spy plenty of fellow queer folks. For an ultra-posh experience, splurge on a suite – many have private infinity pools – at one of the three plush Aman Resorts properties on the island.

## Hong Kong

The chichi Central district of this favoured getaway of international jetsetters is packed with opulent hotels – the Peninsula, Rosewood, Landmark Mandarin Oriental and Shangri-La to name a few. It also boasts a trendy club scene that makes it one of Asia's top destinations for gay singles, and it enjoys a gorgeous setting overlooking Victoria Harbour. You'll find exclusive boutiques at the many high-end shopping plazas, such as Elements (beneath the Ritz-Carlton), Pacific Place and IFC. Worn out from all that retail? Book a luxurious massage at Angsana Spa by Banyan Tree.

## Langkawi

Like Bali, Langkawi is in a Muslim country with a poor track record on LGBTQ rights, but Malaysia's 99-island archipelago in the Malacca Strait — nearly at the Thai border — has nevertheless become one of South-East Asia's favourite luxury gay beach destinations. Langkawi's secluded islands abound with stunning beaches and lush rainforests, and are home to several plush, gay-welcoming international resorts, including the Four Seasons, the St. Regis and the Ritz-Carlton.

## Los Angeles

Roll like a movie star in what might just be the chicest 'gaybourhood' in the world, West Hollywood, where you may very well spot a celebrity or two holding court by the pool of a sceney urban resort — maybe 1 Hotel, Petit Ermitage or the infamous hideaway of the stars, Chateau Marmont, whose distinguished guests have included a roll call of queer icons: Dorothy Parker, James Dean, Annie Leibowitz, Jean-Michel Basquiat and many more. Even many of the top gay hangouts, such as the Abbey and Saint Felix, have a conspicuously monied vibe. WeHo borders the modish boutiques and champagne bars of Beverly Hills, and it's just a short hop to the seaside allure of Santa Monica and Malibu.

## Miami

South Florida's cultural melting pot abounds with ritzy diversions. To clarify, there's the city of Miami, with its shiny high-rise hotel towers, the Mandarin Oriental and the Four Seasons among them. And then there's the separate municipality of Miami Beach, just across Biscayne Bay and stretched out along a prime piece of oceanfront that's home to the voguish LGBTQ scene of South Beach, where you can treat yourself to an overnight stay at the intimate Villa Casa Casuarina (Gianni Versace's former home), or at one of the splendidly restored Art Deco hotels, like the National and the Delano, the frequent sites of fashion shoots and A-list parties.

## Nice and the Côte d'Azur

Famous for its discreetly affluent hilltop villages, celeb-frequented beachfront hotels, rarefied yachting culture and ethereal Mediterranean cuisine, Provence's French Riviera stretches from the sculpted inlets around Saint-Tropez to film-centric Cannes and artsy Antibes and to the Roman city of Nice, the region's queer capital, with friendly bars as well as elegant hotels such as the Negresco and the Belle Époque Boscolo Exedra. But the whole region is popular with everyone from luxury-loving solo travellers to romance-seeking same-sex couples.

> The whole region is popular with everyone from luxury-loving solo travellers to romance-seeking same-sex couples.

## Tulum

Over the past 30 years, this once-sleepy Mexican fishing village on the site of fascinating Mayan ruins has become far more fashionable and exclusive than its bigger and brasher cousin, Cancún, 130 kilometres (80 miles) up the coast. Despite the spate of fashionable boutique hotels and eco-resorts that have popped up mostly along Tulum's beachfront Zona Hotelera – architectural gems like La Valise, Azulik and Be Tulum – this tropical community with about 20,000 year-round residents remains fairly low-key. It's arguably the cushiest destination in a country with several iconic ones, including the Pacific Coast towns of Cabo San Lucas and Punta Mita.

### The 5-and-2 plan

Unless it's work-related and someone else is footing the bill, my partner and I travel on a fairly modest budget. But we also find ways to treat ourselves to plush experiences. My favourite strategy is what I call the 5-and-2 plan. If you're going away for a week, book the first five nights someplace economical, and then use the money you saved to splurge for someplace swanky the final two nights. This can be far more rewarding than staying at one mid-priced but not especially interesting hotel the entire time. We apply this approach to dining and attractions, too – eating cheaply, buying groceries and cooking occasionally in inexpensive Airbnbs much of the trip, but then splurging on two or three really amazing meals or some other high-ticket treat, like a spa treatment.

### Use points

Accumulating points through airline, hotel and other loyalty programs – or by signing up for a co-branded credit card – can sometimes yield impressive rewards. Credit card sign-up bonuses can be especially generous – enough to score three or four nights at an upscale hotel, or a pair of business-class airline tickets. You can also use points to upgrade or purchase seats in premium cabins.

### Prix-fixe meals

If you're dining out someplace special, ask if there's a prix-fixe or tasting menu (with wine pairings, if you're into that). These tend to be more cost-effective than ordering à la carte, and they often showcase a chef's most creative dishes. Even at restaurants that don't officially offer this option, we sometimes ask if we can pay a fixed amount per person for the chef to come up with a menu for us. It's especially fun doing this with friends and sharing everything family-style.

## Spa days

To make the most of a spa experience, set aside at least three hours, even if you book only an hour-long treatment. For the cost of a massage, we've sometimes been able to enjoy an entire afternoon in a gorgeous spa, chilling out ahead of our treatments in a reception room or working out in a state-of-the-art gym, then afterwards swimming, lazing on a sun deck or decompressing in a steam room, sauna or hot tub.

.

We've had a blast spending time with friends.

.

## Friends with benefits

For every person you add to your travel group, the cost of accommodation and activities — tours, taxi rides, car rentals — can drop significantly. This rule applies especially to vacation rentals. We often find another couple or several friends to go in with us on Airbnbs and sometimes score far swankier digs than had we gone it alone — and we've had a blast spending time with friends.

# Where the wild things are

I make it a policy not to corner innocent bystanders at cocktail parties and regale them with tales of my travels — at least not unless I'm prompted. But the one trip I've taken over the past 20 years that I simply won't shut up about is the wildlife safari I experienced in the enormous **Kruger National Park** in the north-east corner of South Africa, which is by far the most LGBTQ-affirming country on the continent.

A friend and I stayed in a spectacular glass-walled suite at the **Singita Lebombo Lodge**, and we went out on game drives each day, during which we came within astonishingly close range of lions, elephants, leopards, rhinos, giraffes and more. I can neither confirm nor deny that part of the fun included being smuggled over a border fence into Mozambique for a hike, and having to help push our small plane off the gravel airstrip after it blew a tyre during our landing. But suffice to say, it was the trip of a lifetime.

Singita is one of the world's best safari companies, and all of its cushy lodges are exceptional, but there are dozens of other companies that operate in the park. And for LGBTQ travellers planning a safari, I do recommend sticking either with South Africa or possibly Botswana, Mozambique, Namibia or Rwanda, as to varying degrees these countries have made strides regarding gay rights in recent years. Other major safari destinations — such as Kenya, Tanzania, Uganda, Zambia and Zimbabwe — have both laws and attitudes that are problematic.

Whether it's to celebrate your honeymoon or just to treat yourself to a truly special adventure, there are few better ways to pamper yourself than by spending a couple of nights in a truly over-the-top-opulent suite.

The priciest room at a hotel isn't always the most romantic. Suites named 'Presidential' or 'Penthouse' are often booked by dignitaries and have extra bedrooms and entertainment spaces — amenities you and your sweetheart probably don't need, unless you're travelling with a secret service detail or hosting a board meeting.

There are three things I ask when seeking out an uber-posh crash pad. Are the views — be it an electrifying city skyline or a craggy volcanic peak — truly bewitching? Is there a breathtaking water feature, such as a private plunge pool on the balcony or a steam shower large enough to accommodate a volleyball team? Is there a smartly designed kitchen, or at least a wet bar with a good-size fridge, to store and prepare some fancy snacks?

It's nice if the property has world-class dining and spa amenities, too, but sometimes the ultimate romantic retreat is simply a quiet, secluded cabin on a rocky promontory overlooking the sea. Here are some of my favourite mind-blowing hideaways.

### Cliff House, Lifetime Private Retreat, Kangaroo Island, South Australia

One of the most amazing places I've ever awakened is in this hideaway's circular-tower bedroom, taking in sweeping vistas of Snelling Beach and Investigator Strait. It's on Kangaroo Island, famous for wildlife viewing (not just kangaroos, but koalas, platypus, echidnas and sea lions). One of a few vacation homes at this stunning compound, the three-bedroom Cliff House has a full kitchen and an outdoor infinity Jacuzzi. And yes, there's a landing pad for your helicopter.

### Crescent Pavilion Suite, the Berkeley Hotel, London

Sure, you could actually buy a pretty nice car for what it costs to spend the night in the André Fu–designed penthouse at this storied 1867 Knightsbridge hotel, but, if you can afford it, you're in for the treat of a lifetime. Naturally, rates include round-the-clock butler services and transfer via a Mercedes V-Class sedan.

### Bay Tower Room, Lands End Inn, Provincetown

The most dramatic of several remarkable rooms in an eccentric 1904 mansion in Provincetown's hilly West End, the octagonal Bay Tower — with its striking cupola-dome ceiling — affords panoramic views of Cape Cod Bay and has two huge balconies.

### Penthouse Suite, Casa Cupula, Puerto Vallarta

A huge indoor shower along with a smaller outdoor shower, a Jacuzzi and a rooftop terrace with your own infinity pool provide plenty of romantic ways for you and a friend — or friends — to cool off or warm up at this gay-owned boutique resort high on a hill overlooking Bahía de Banderas.

### Louis Leonowens Pool Suite, 137 Pillars House, Chiang Mai

French doors lead from the graciously appointed bedrooms of these colonial-chic suites out to a peaceful garden with a shower and private pool. This intimate inn also has one of the classiest restaurants in the mountainous northern Thailand city of Chiang Mai, an artsy and chill ecotourism-minded alternative to frenetic Bangkok.

### Canopy Suite, Wickaninnish Inn, Tofino, British Columbia

In this huge, richly furnished room in the remote, pristine Vancouver Island village of Tofino, a glowing fireplace and soaring floor-to-ceiling windows frame the view of massive waves crashing over Chesterman Beach.

### Terrace Suite, InterContinental Mark Hopkins Hotel, San Francisco

With a glass-enclosed terrace offering eye-popping views of one of the world's most glorious cities, this ample 15th-floor suite is the ultimate San Francisco treat. The Mark Hopkins was built in 1926 atop Nob Hill, one of the fanciest addresses in California.

*If you can afford it, you're in for the treat of a lifetime.*

# Fun on a budget

.

If you've made it to this point of the
book, you've hopefully come up with
a long list of places you're eager to
visit. For the majority of us, there's
just this one little impediment to
dropping everything and roaming
the globe: money.

How can we afford to visit all of these fabulous places, some of them quite spendy or reached by an expensive flight? Fortunately, you needn't blow a small fortune to travel someplace exciting, picturesque and gay-sensible. There are amazing, affordable vacations to be had all over the world, and there are also ways to make higher-end destinations more affordable (*see* p. 122).

What you won't find in this chapter is a long list of travel tips on how to travel on a shoestring budget. You've probably seen these click-baity advice stories online. Some of this advice is pretty useful, some not so much. *Fit all of your clothing into one small carry-on to avoid baggage fees*. Please, I need separate pairs of footwear for clubbing, walking around town, hiking, beachcombing and working out in the gym – I can't even fit all of my shoes into a single carry-on. *Book the tiniest rental car possible*. This might work for a short weekend trip without much driving, but I love road-tripping. Also, see above: how are my partner and I supposed to cram four suitcases into the back of a tiny two-door rental car? *Be prepared to haggle for the best price*. Personally, I'd rather stay home than turn every transaction into a tiresome price negotiation.

We all have different ideas about what we're willing to sacrifice in order to save a little money. I'm perfectly happy to travel midweek, use public transport, buy some local groceries instead of always dining out and visit museums at weird times to avoid high admission prices. I carry credit cards that don't charge international exchange fees, and I spend time online shopping around for the best air, car rental and hotel deals. Here are a few more ideas.

## PAY ATTENTION TO CURRENCY EXCHANGE RATES

One simple way to save money is to visit places where your currency is stronger than the local currency. Some countries — Argentina, Mexico and Vietnam, for example — have had favourable exchange rates relative to much of the rest of the world for years. In other cases, the rates between currencies can fluctuate or even flip-flop in a matter of several years.

Check which countries are the most favourable when you're deciding where to holiday. If you find yourself someplace where your own currency goes a long way, try to be humble about your good fortune. I've overheard visitors from North America squeal while perusing the menu of a fancy restaurant in Mexico City. But for residents who earn their income in the local currency, dining out in Mexico City is no bargain. It's understandable that you're delighted about the low cost of a steak in Buenos Aires or a massage in Saigon, but perhaps tactfully keep your excitement to yourself.

## USE A VACATION RENTAL SERVICE

The success of **Airbnb** and other marketplace-oriented vacation services has sometimes had unintended negative consequences related to gentrification and rising housing costs, but there's no denying these sites have also made it easier to find cheap rooms in even exorbitant cities.

While Airbnb has strived to create an inclusive marketplace free of discrimination, it's still possible to run up against renters who don't warmly welcome LGBTQ guests. When I book on Airbnb, I always send the owner a note briefly introducing myself and my partner. I've occasionally had my reservation declined, always with an innocuous explanation. Was it actually because we're a gay couple? I'll never know, but if so, I'd rather have been turned away in advance than treated inhospitably on arrival.

If you're concerned, consider staying only at properties with the Instant Book option, which requires owners to accept reservations immediately, without first learning anything about their guests, or book only an unhosted accommodation in which you have the whole place to yourself.

Or use a vacation rental agency geared specifically to LGBTQ travellers. The most established of these is **misterb&b**, which originated with a mostly gay-male focus but has expanded rapidly and now caters to the entire LGBTQ community. The site has more than one million listings in over 200 countries, and detailed owner profiles make it easy to find hosts who match your exact level of wanting to interact and socialise together. Like Airbnb, misterb&b also offers guest experiences, anything from local guided tours to hosted dinners.

The cheapest of these homestay services is **Couchsurfing.com**, a site based on the 'gift economy' principle, meaning that members don't charge guests anything to host them. Just log on, create a profile and start browsing, or consider becoming a host yourself.

Whatever lifehacks and inside tips you might read about budget travel, the most effective way to save a bundle is simply to go somewhere that offers a lot of value. Lots of big cities with vibrant gay scenes come to mind, including several that have been covered elsewhere in this book, such as Cape Town (*see* p. 60), Istanbul (*see* p. 65), Hanoi (*see* p. 106), Bangkok (*see* p. 58) and Mexico City (*see* p. 67). Here are some other great queer budget options.

### Buenos Aires

Argentina has one of Latin America's weakest currencies, so its sophisticated, bustling capital city is an easy place to score favourable deals on wine, leather goods and fashion – even in the ritzy Recoleta district. And restaurants and hotels are affordable, too, particularly the many indie hotels and Airbnbs in charming outlying neighbourhoods, such as Palermo Viejo and San Telmo, which abound with gay nightspots, trendy bistros and hip boutiques.

Use a vacation rental agency geared specifically to LGBTQ travellers.

## Bogotá

In terms of LGBTQ rights and popularity with gay travellers, Colombia is a rising star. It has anti-discrimination laws and same-sex marriage, and travel safety has improved tremendously in recent years, too. With a lively gay scene centred around the upscale Chapinero neighbourhood, the high-altitude capital city of Bogotá is easy to visit cheaply. Led by an openly lesbian mayor, this animated metropolis of about 7.5 million has exceptional museums, dramatic Andes Mountains views and impressive retail offerings where bargains abound. From Bogotá, you can also find cheap flights to Colombia's other, even less expensive LGBTQ hubs – including Medellín, another mountainous metropolis with a happening food scene, edgy street graffiti and pulsing gay clubs, and Cartagena, the charming colonial port city with colourfully painted historic buildings and palm-fringed white-sand Caribbean beaches.

## Guadalajara

Sometimes referred to as the 'San Francisco of Mexico' for its super-friendly and festive gay scene, the country's second-largest city exudes creative energy. It's a wonderful place to experience mariachi and folk-music culture, drink fine tequila, shop for authentic arts and crafts, devour superb regional cuisine, admire beautifully restored Spanish Colonial architecture and mingle with exceedingly friendly locals. And travel costs are as little as half what you might expect in Mexico City, which is itself a relative bargain compared with the rest of North America. It's also a short flight or half-day bus ride from famously gay Puerto Vallarta.

## Las Vegas

For all its glitzy, and sometimes gaudy, excess, Sin City is actually easy to enjoy on the cheap. It helps that travel costs are heavily subsidised by the gaming industry. The gay bars are a lot of fun, too – they're usually open 24/7 and offer enticing drink specials. Las Vegas also has cheap flights from many big cities. Of course, you can easily turn your Vegas vacation into a high-rolling romp, especially if you get soaked at the casino. Springing for Cirque du Soleil tickets or a hotel suite with a gold-plated toilet isn't going to help your bottom line either. If you start haemorrhaging money, get as far as you can from the pulsing neon on the Las Vegas Strip and spend your time and money in the hip and emerging downtown Las Vegas Arts District, eating your way through the amazing and cheap 'Little Asia' restaurant scene on Spring Mountain Road, or staying at one of the dapper but affordable outlying resorts, such as Red Rock Casino or M Resort.

## Lisbon

Portugal is one of southern Europe's greatest bargains, and the vibrant capital city of Lisbon, with its unpretentious and friendly LGBTQ community and impressive culinary chops, has a tremendous amount going for it. The climate is warm and relatively dry, which you'll appreciate when sunbathing at gay-popular, clothing-optional Beach 19, just a half-hour drive from the city centre. Set on the Atlantic Coast at the mouth of the Tagus River, this hilly ancient port city with Roman ruins and striking museums abounds with good hotel deals and affordable restaurants. Pro tip: the country's other cool LGBTQ city, Porto, is even less expensive than Lisbon and is just a three-hour drive up the coast.

## Montréal

One of the New World's most old-world cities, impossibly charming, diverse and inclusive Montréal probably shouldn't be as affordable as it is. If you're keen on French language and culture, it's also a lot cheaper to get here from elsewhere in North America than flying all the way to Paris. Canada's second-largest city gets bonus points for single travellers and clubbers, thanks to the saucy saunas and fantastic LGBTQ bars in the happening Gay Village, which also boasts lovely and affordable inns and vacation rentals. Montréal's astonishingly good restaurants – especially in foodie neighbourhoods like Little Burgundy and the adjoining Mile End and Mile-Ex districts – offer excellent value, too.

## New Orleans

The cost of travel ranges considerably in the US, but you'll get the best bang for your buck in the South. And while it has a reputation for backward attitudes about queer people, the South is also home to several highly progressive cities, including Atlanta, Houston, Nashville and Dallas. But the ultimate queer vacation spot in this part of the world is spirited, diverse New Orleans, which does have its share of spendy hotels and restaurants but also offers scores of reasonably priced options, such as lesbian-owned Willa Jean, helmed by James Beard–award winning pastry chef Kelly Fields. With plenty of wild but welcoming gay bars that will pour you a daquiri any time of day or night, it's a great town for partying, especially if you come during Mardi Gras or the fabulously queer five-day Southern Decadence party in early September.

## Prague

Quite possibly the most popular LGBTQ getaway in Central Europe, this walkable city with meticulously preserved medieval architecture and a booming queer nightlife is remarkably affordable. Straddling the Vltava River and buzzing with romantic terrace cafes and old-school restaurants, Prague is easy to navigate on foot but also has an efficient and cheap metro system – this comes in handy when wanting to get from the historic Old Town (Staré Město) to the heart of the gay nightlife district in Vinohrady. It won't cost you anything to stroll across the iconic Charles Bridge, which offers stunning views of the skyline and Prague Castle.

Canada's second-largest city gets bonus points for single travellers and clubbers.

# Back to school

When I'm looking for engaging places to travel that offer the perfect confluence of affordability, creative energy and queerness, I often look to university towns, which can be a great value as long as you avoid graduation weekends, big sports events and the like.

In these youthful, educated communities, even if you don't find a gay bar per se, you're likely to encounter a very accepting and queer vibe — including greater awareness of and support for transgender people — and a good range of funky boutiques, cheap restaurants and affordable accommodation. And the arts scenes are often amazing — acclaimed university museums, indie theatres and cinemas, lectures and author readings.

Here are some of the world's best university towns for LGBTQ travel and having plenty to see and do:

- **Ann Arbor**, Michigan, US
- **Athens**, Georgia, US
- **Berkeley**, California, US
- **Bologna**, Italy
- **Boulder**, Colorado, US
- **Dunedin**, New Zealand
- **Guanajuato**, Mexico
- **Kingston**, Ontario, Canada
- **Leiden**, Netherlands
- **Madison**, Wisconsin, US

- **Mannheim**, Germany
- **Montpellier**, France
- **Oxford**, England
- **Raleigh-Durham-Chapel Hill**, North Carolina, US
- **St Andrews**, Scotland
- **Uppsala**, Sweden
- **Valparaíso**, Chile
- **Wollongong**, Australia.

# Travelling safely

In much of the world, laws and attitudes concerning sexual orientation have improved dramatically in just the past decade or two. It wasn't so long ago that travel for gay people meant trying to suss out a few remote, nonconformist or 'artsy' resort communities and urban neighbourhoods where queer people could (discreetly) congregate. You still risked being harassed or beaten up by walking down the wrong alley, or being arrested and publicly shamed for being in a bar or park during a police raid. The calculation behind choosing where to holiday, and with whom, was based more on self-preservation than having fun.

Travelling openly with, or in search of, a lover of the same gender came with enormous risks. If you were also part of another marginalised community – based on gender, race or economic circumstances – holidaying openly as a queer person felt even more fraught.

It's a big deal that so much has improved – that on six continents you can visit amazing places that welcome LGBTQ visitors enthusiastically. That you can celebrate a same-sex wedding. That you can meet other queer people at cafes, bars, community centres and countless other venues, as well as by using smartphone apps.

## Navigating hostile territory

Although the world is becoming more LGBTQ welcoming, queer people of colour and transgender people are still far too likely to be discriminated against even in ostensibly progressive countries. Furthermore, about 70 countries still criminalise same-sex sexual activity and, even in some places where it's legal, queer people are harassed by authorities or forbidden to hold Pride rallies. Yet deciding where to travel isn't always as simple as considering local LGBTQ laws and attitudes. Many factors determine our willingness to visit potentially inhospitable places.

In this book, I didn't include places where LGBTQ people face extreme danger, such as Iran, Brunei, Nigeria and Saudi

Arabia. That's not to say there aren't valid reasons to travel where gay people face major risks. Maybe you've always wanted to see Egypt's Pyramids of Giza, for instance. If you do travel someplace intolerant, consider booking through a gay-owned travel agency with safe local contacts, and be prepared to hide your sexual orientation.

In some destinations, evaluating LGBTQ tolerance is complicated. I've included some less-inclusive places – such as Istanbul, Bali, Langkawi and parts of the US – because I feel their positive attributes outweigh the negatives. Other places that I omitted because of their poor LGBTQ reputations nevertheless have surprisingly significant, if discreet, gay followings. These include Singapore, Sri Lanka, Ghana, Kenya, the Maldives, the United Arab Emirates, Morocco and a number of (mostly former British) Caribbean islands, such as Antigua, Barbados, Jamaica, Grenada and St Lucia. The situation may be gradually improving in some of these countries, but you should still approach them with caution.

Travelling to less welcoming places can also be a conscious political or humanitarian act – a way to help stamp out prejudice and change attitudes by being open and getting to know locals. This can also be a meaningful way to support LGBTQ residents and queer-supportive businesses in conservative areas.

But where you travel is a personal decision and if you prefer not to spend money in LGBTQ-hostile places, that's a valid choice, too. If unsure about a destination, ask around and search online. The International Gay and Lesbian Travel Association (IGLTA), a huge online network of LGBTQ-welcoming businesses and tourism offices, is a great resource.

If you can't get a clear sense of a destination's gay vibe, think carefully about your expectations. Can you still have fun if you and your partner must pretend not to be a couple, or if it's too dangerous to go to gay bars or use dating apps? There's no right or wrong answer. Most of us can imagine when we might be willing to make this sacrifice – and when we wouldn't. For LGBTQ travellers, the world is imperfect, but we've also come a long way.

# About the author

Andrew Collins has been writing about travel and food for a variety of both LGBTQ and mainstream magazines, websites and guidebook publishers for the past 30 years. He also teaches travel and food writing online for Gotham Writers Workshop, in New York City.

Congenitally incapable of sitting still, he spends more than half the year travelling, and has a particular fondness for national parks, offbeat small towns, and dive bars and roadside cafes. He usually travels with his wonderful partner, Fernando Nocedal, to whom he dedicates this book.

He and Fernando divide their time between the Coyoacán district of Mexico City, where they reside with their two absurdly friendly cats, and a cottage on a tiny lake in rural New Hampshire, where they fall asleep at night to the haunting calls of loons and barred owls.

You can find more of his work at AndrewsTraveling.com, and follow him on Instagram at TravelAndrew.

# About the illustrator

Wenjia Tang is a freelance illustrator who graduated from Maryland Institute College of Art in 2017. She was born in south-east China, and went to the United States for high school when she was 15. She loves all kinds of animals, and lives with a cat in Manhattan, New York.

Her work has been recognised by American Illustration, Society of Illustrators, *Communication Arts*, AOI, *3x3 Magazine* and more.

Published in 2021 by Hardie Grant Explore,
a division of Hardie Grant Publishing

Hardie Grant Explore (Melbourne)
Wurundjeri Country
Building 1, 658 Church Street
Richmond, Victoria 3121

Hardie Grant Explore (Sydney)
Gadigal Country
Level 7, 45 Jones Street
Ultimo, NSW 2007

www.hardiegrant.com/au/travel

A catalogue record for this
book is available from the
National Library of Australia

Hardie Grant acknowledges the Traditional Owners of the country
on which we work, the Wurundjeri people of the Kulin nation and the
Gadigal people of the Eora nation, and recognises their continuing
connection to the land, waters and culture. We pay our respects to
their Elders past, present and emerging.

Destination Pride
ISBN 9781741176971

10 9 8 7 6 5 4 3 2 1

**Publisher**
Melissa Kayser

**Senior editor**
Megan Cuthbert

**Design**
Michelle Mackintosh

**Project editor**
Alexandra Payne

**Proofreader**
Rosanna Dutson

**Typesetting**
Megan Ellis

Colour reproduction by Megan Ellis and Splitting Image Colour Studio
Printed and bound in China by LEO Paper Products LTD.

The paper this book is printed on is certified
against the Forest Stewardship Council®
Standards and other sources. FSC® promotes
environmentally responsible, socially beneficial
and economically viable management of the
world's forests.

MIX
Paper from
responsible sources
www.fsc.org   FSC® C020056